"I had the pleasure of listening to Jennifer Kennedy Dean share a brief morning devotion on prayer. The depth, insight, and truth of her words spoke to me in a powerful way. A few minutes with Jennifer challenged me and changed my praying life. With *Live a Praying Life* Anniversary Edition, I can engage in more than a few minutes. I can look forward to 13 weeks of learning and growing and communing with the Lord."

—Kendra Smiley, conference speaker and author of *Journey of a Strong-Willed Child*

"A great prayer study to grow your intimacy with the Father and gain confidence that He hears and answers prayer."

—Fern Nichols, founder and president, Moms In Touch International

"*Live a Praying Life* is a true classic and an immensely valuable book on prayer. Reading it, applying its truths, and doing the accompanying study will infuse your life with faith and bring a new dimension to your prayer life, helping you to discover a more vibrant relationship with Christ."

—Cheri Fuller, speaker and author of *The One Year Book of Praying Through the Bible, A Busy Woman's Guide to Prayer,* and *Mother-Daughter Duet*

"I have used *Live a Praying Life* in my personal study and I've recommended it many, many times. I love the simple way Jennifer Kennedy Dean explains biblical truths in a way that excites me and inspires my prayer life. I've grown in my understanding of Jesus and I've been drawn into His presence through this study. Highly recommended!"

—Tricia Goyer, author of *Blue Like Play Dough*

"Anyone seeking a deeper understanding of the heart of the One who calls us into His presence, the One who prompts us to bring our words (some inexpressible) to the throne within His chamber, will know immediately upon opening this book they have struck gold."

—Eva Marie Everson, author of *Shadow of Dreams* and *Summon the Shadows*

Live a Praying Life

Open Your Life to **God's Power** and Provision

JENNIFER KENNEDY DEAN

NEW HOPE®
PUBLISHERS
Gospel-Centered. Missions-Driven.

Birmingham, Alabama

New Hope® Publishers
P. O. Box 12065
Birmingham, AL 35202-2065
www.newhopepublishers.com
New Hope Publishers is a division of WMU®.

Library of Congress Cataloging-in-Publication Data

Dean, Jennifer Kennedy.
  Live a praying life : open your life to God's power and provision / By
Jennifer Kennedy Dean.
    p. cm.
  ISBN 978-1-59669-291-6 (sc)
  1. Prayer--Christianity. I. Title.
  BV215.D34 2010
  248.3'2076--dc22
                    2010016232

ISBN-10: 1-59669-291-X
ISBN-13: 978-1-59669-291-6

N104148 • 0517 • 5M11

To Daddy
Don W. Kennedy

You made it easy for me to believe that I have a heavenly Father
who lavishes undeserved love on me
and who keeps me as the apple of His eye.

How great is the love the Father has lavished on us,
that we should be called children of God! —1 John 3:1

With all my heart, I thank the many, many people who, over these years, have listened to me teach, read my work, and asked the hard questions. You have challenged me and encouraged me as I have honed this manuscript over the years.

Jennifer Kennedy Dean

Section One: The Purpose of Prayer

Section Two: The Process of Prayer

Section Three: The Promise of Prayer

Section Four: The Practice of Prayer

Appendixes

I want to find the precise words that will convey to you what this anniversary edition of *Live a Praying Life* means to me. This is the message that has consumed me all of my adult life. In 1973, when I was 20 years old, events in my life forced me into a crisis of faith that drove me either to seek out answers and understanding about prayer, or to abandon it altogether. I described this crisis in *Fueled by Faith*:

MY FAITH PASSAGE

The summer following my graduation from high school, my only brother, who was two years my junior and my best friend, was diagnosed with a rare and deadly form of leukemia. Because of my mother's strong prayer network and my parents' absolute faith in God, Roger's illness was covered in prayer continually. We firmly believed that his body would be restored and even when his symptoms worsened that belief did not waver. Throughout the year of his illness, we saw many instances of healing—times when the doctors gave up hope, or when a new and serious symptom would emerge. When he was first diagnosed, the immediate life-threatening danger was a large cantaloupe-sized tumor that was crushing his bronchial tubes, making it difficult for him to breathe and pushing his organs out of place so that his heart was beside his stomach. It was already at such a stage that Roger's death could be only days away. Our church opened its doors to the community for prayer and word is that a standing-room-only crowd attended. Our family was at the hospital 100 miles away, but many who were present report that there was a discernable, almost physical, sense of the Lord's presence. By the next morning, the tumor had shrunk by half. A week later it was gone entirely. Time and time again miraculous healing of symptoms occurred and it affirmed our faith. Yet, a year after his disease had been diagnosed, my sweet brother died, the withered shell of his body lying in a hospital bed.

As sick as he was, the news of his death was the last thing I expected to hear. Yet, at that moment, what I can only describe as a blanket of peace covered me. My family members all report the same experience. I did not know the Lord and His ways well at that time. But I did not have to do or believe anything to receive His love that literally overpowered what the responses of my flesh would have been. His intervention in every detail of the situation continued to be obvious as He comforted us in supernatural ways.

Later, left-brain analytical thinker that God has created me to be, I began to wonder, "If all that prayer for his healing was going on, and Roger died anyway, what good was prayer?" It compelled me into a search for answers and understanding that has defined the call of God on my life. God produced something eternal through Roger's death. His life was a seed that fell into the ground to produce a harvest.

When I write a book or a Bible study, the content comes from what I have studied and sought out in answer to my own questions and needs. I write to myself. When the insights that have changed my life find resonance in someone else's life, it is encouraging and gratifying to me. Since I believe that *Live a Praying Life* is the foundational message of my life, I am thrilled that it is still reaching others with the truths that God has worked into the fiber of my being and worked out in the rough-and-tumble of living life on planet Earth.

WHAT'S NEW?

Since *Live a Praying Life* was first published, I have had many opportunities to road test the truth. In light of that, I'll share new insights and experiences each week throughout this anniversary edition (see "Anniversary Thoughts," beginning on p. 31). I've also included at the end of this book my testimony about how these principles sustained me and proved true through the experience of losing my husband to brain cancer in 2005 (p. 216). And in a new appendix I list some of my favorite books on prayer (p. 220).

As I stated in the original introduction, one of my goals in writing this book is to give you the opportunity to pray, not just think about prayer. So I'm excited to let you know about a new journaling resource, *Live a Praying Life Journal*, which would be an excellent accompaniment through your study or can stand on its own as a prayer journal. The journal offers plenty of room to pen your thoughts and features powerful Scripture to ponder accompanied by brief thoughts from several of my books. In addition, to enhance your learning experience, a *Live a Praying Life* DVD Leader Kit Anniversary Edition is available featuring a brand-new live recording of my teaching and much more. Finally, you will find other resources, many of them free, at my Web site, www.prayinglife.org.

I'm glad you are joining me on my never-ending journey to live a praying life.

I grew up in a praying family. From earliest childhood, I was encouraged to commit everything to God through prayer. Nothing was either too important or too insignificant to leave in God's hands. My parents did not teach me about prayer with their words, but with their lives. They had more than "a prayer time"—a section of their days set aside for praying. Instead, prayer permeated and controlled every aspect of their lives.

Prayer, I later came to realize, can be an activity or it can be a life. You can think of it in terms of "my prayer life," as you would say "my home life," or "my work life"—as if prayer were one compartment among many.

But I knew that prayer as a task or an activity would not meet the deep yearning I had to know God. It was not a prayer life I wanted, but *a praying life*—a life of ongoing and continual interaction with God. Andrew Murray has said, "Answered prayer is the interchange of love between the Father and His child." I want an uninterrupted flow of love between the Father and me. Isn't that what you want? Isn't your heart crying out for that?

You see, there is an undercurrent of prayer always active in a believer's life. The Spirit of Christ is within you crying out, "Abba, Father" (Galatians 4:6). To put it in today's language, He is calling out, "Daddy! Daddy!" The Spirit is always praying the Father's will, and the Spirit is housed in you (Romans 8:9, 11, 15, 26–27, and 1 Corinthians 6:19). At some level, in every believer, prayer is always happening. *The praying life is Christ.* It is the life of Jesus Christ operating in you. The key to learning to live a praying life is this: learn how, more and more often, to tap into the undercurrent of prayer, the active presence of Jesus in you. Join your voice with His in harmonious prayer.

When I became a young adult, I realized that a praying life was not built on information communicated from one person to another, but on a life-absorbing relationship with God. I sensed the difference between a prayer life and a *praying life*, and I knew which one I craved. I knew that there was only One who could teach me to pray—who could be my Prayer Teacher. To Him I brought my inadequacy and my hungry heart. "Lord," I cried, "I know how to say prayers, but I don't know how to pray. Teach me to pray!"

In response to my heart's cry to teach me deep truths about prayer, God began to open His Word to me in new ways. Familiar passages took on fresh meaning. Dull, dry passages pulsed with new life. I felt myself being "taught by the Lord" (Isaiah 54:13). To this day, some thirty years since I embarked on this

When I became a young adult, I realized that a praying life was not built on information communicated from one person to another, but on a life-absorbing relationship with God.

soul-quest, it is still new. Each time I discover a concept, He brings me opportunities to put it to the test. The words of the Scriptures shape my life and define my experiences. Slowly but surely, He is building my life into a praying life.

As I submitted myself to God for instruction in prayer, He seemed to ask me, "Jennifer, why do you want to learn to pray?" I knew all the "right" answers, but they had a hollow, false ring to them. My experience must have been similar to Peter's. How surprised he was when Jesus did not accept his glib answer to the question, "Peter, do you love Me?" Each time Jesus asked, Peter must have been forced to look deeper inside his heart for the true answer.

That is always God's starting place—your truth. No matter how ugly your truth is, He can work from it. What He can't work from is pretense. As He had with Peter, God peeled back the layers of my practiced, memorized, other people's answers until my truth emerged. And my truth was not pretty. "Father, I want to know how to pray so that I will know how to get You to do *what* I want You to do *when* I want You to do it. I hope to learn how to make the best possible use of prayer for my benefit."

Once I reached that point of honesty, I knew my course was set. God could work with me now because He could begin with my weakness. At the point of my weakness, His strength would be put on display. My Prayer Teacher could begin by teaching me a new purpose for prayer.

This book tells of my journey so far. But the journey never ends. Every single day I learn something new about prayer, or I learn something in a deeper way. It is my hope that when others read what I have learned and the inner changes that have occurred, they will be inspired to sit at the Master's feet.

Think back to your childhood. What were your impressions of prayer? What part did it play in your life? Do you remember any experiences with prayer that helped define it for you, either positively or negatively?

Who was the first person whose life of prayer made an impression on you?

Who are the people in your life who have modeled a relationship with God that made you realize there was something deeper?

Write out your own heart's cry to your Prayer Teacher. What is your prayer as you study *Live a Praying Life*?

How to Use This Book

You can use this book on your own, or you can join others who have the same desire to learn the deep truths about prayer. It is designed so that you work through the material over the course of 13 weeks. The material is divided into daily sections, five days for each week.

My goal is to cause you to handle the Scripture and to think through the points carefully. You will get the most benefit from this book if you leave behind what you have always thought of as the "right" or "acceptable" answers and be open to fresh truth. Let the Spirit of God energize and enlighten your reasoning ability. Think! Ask the hard questions. Don't accept anything as truth except what is spoken in the whole Word of God.

In the first few lessons you may find that you are "unlearning" some false concepts. You may find that your prayer doctrine has been infiltrated with "prayer myths." You may find this somewhat jarring or disorienting. But if you will stick with it, you will begin to put the pieces back together. You will see that subtle error has been robbing you of all the power available through prayer. You will find the whole truth, and prayer will make sense.

You see, I believe that God is calling us to become "prayer technicians." Here's what I mean: I am fairly proficient in using my computer—as long as it does what I thought it would do. But sometimes I push the right button and the wrong thing happens on the screen. I get messages like: "This program has performed an illegal operation and will be shut down," or "A fatal error has occurred." When I push the right button but the wrong thing happens, I'm at a loss. I don't know where to go from there. I'm not a computer technician. I don't understand a computer's inner workings. The inner workings of a computer are "secret wisdom" to me.

In prayer, many of us have pushed the right button but the wrong thing happened. Since we have only learned the outward appearances and not the inner workings, we're at a loss. But God wants to train us to be "prayer technicians." He wants to reveal the "secret wisdom" (1 Corinthians 2:7), the inner workings of prayer.

As you work through the material, you will have the opportunity to process it in reflective and probing questions and interactive exercises. Sometimes the questions are designed to help you identify misconceptions that you hold. Some of the questions, I hope, will make you chuckle at yourself. Believe me, they are drawn from my own journey. I am often amused at my own earth-based thinking.

One of my goals in writing this book is to give you the opportunity to pray, not just think about prayer. So I have designed a section each day called "Practice a New Way of Praying." These sections are daily prayer journal exercises. Each week we will use a different prayer jump start method. My hope is that you will begin to feel confident in praying and see how many, many forms prayer takes. At the beginning of each week's material, I will give instructions about the week's prayer journaling. At the end of each day's material, you will find a prayer journaling section.

My Prayer for You

Prayer Teacher, thank You for awakening in this person a hunger for You. Spirit of prayer, You who know the mind of God, lead this one into all truth. Great and mighty God, You who invite us to approach You boldly and make audacious requests, grant this child of Yours a grand sense of adventure. Set this beloved one free from anything that would restrict him or her from joyous exploration of all the nooks and crannies, all the secret places, all the hidden riches of Your Kingdom. In Jesus' name we pray. Amen.

Section One

The Purpose of Prayer

The Purpose of Prayer

PRACTICE A NEW WAY OF PRAYING

Pray this prayer every day for a week. Pray it slowly, taking time to consider each word and phrase. Each day, emphasize a different word or phrase. What new insights or understanding do you get as you saturate your heart and mind in this prayer? Make your observation specific to your own situations and concerns. What is God telling you?

Show me your ways, O LORD, teach me your paths; guide me in your truth and teach me, for you are God my Savior, and my hope is in you all day long. —Psalm 25:4–5

DAY ONE

I entrusted myself fully to the Master's teaching. I was committed to this journey, wherever it would take me. I was certain there were answers to the questions that perplexed me. The first question I had to understand was this: Can I change God through prayer? This presented a dilemma for my orderly mind because it seemed to have a pitfall either way. If I can change God, then He's not sovereign. If I can't change God, then what good is prayer?

I realized that in practice, I had prayed as if I could change God. I prayed as if I could open His eyes to new possibilities, awaken love or mercy in Him, or sway Him to my point of view. If I could just say the right words, I thought, or say them in the right order, or say them often enough, or say them with the right amount of fervor—somehow I could get God to do what I thought He should do. I felt that I had to convince God. I felt that I had to prove my need or give Him a reason to answer me. I approached prayer as if God were hoarding blessings and my role was to get Him to release them. It was a draining responsibility—to be clever enough to convince God. It caused my prayer life to be anxiety-driven, always wondering if I had been effective enough to win God over.

In retrospect, I giggle at how I approached God in prayer! As if God were waiting for me to make suggestions for Him to consider. As if, when

I prayed, God said, "Why didn't I think of that? I wonder what other good ideas Jennifer might have for Me?" But at the beginning of my journey, I couldn't see anything else prayer would be *for*. If God already knows what He wants to do, why does He need my prayers?

Think about your prayer life. When you pray, what do you assume happens in heaven?

a. God says, "What a great idea! I'll take that under advisement. Maybe— just maybe—if he can bring Me enough documentation or can make a strong enough case, I'll consider his idea."

b. God says, "The majority of the requests on this matter are leaning in the other direction. I'll have to deny your request. I have to go with the majority."

c. God says, "Someone else got here first."

d. God says, "You've let Me down so many times. What makes you think I would give you anything you asked for? You don't deserve to have your prayers answered."

e. None of the above.

What is your answer to this dilemma: Does prayer change God? If so, can He be sovereign? If not, why should I pray?

Week 1, Day 1
PRACTICE A NEW WAY OF PRAYING

What is God saying to you?

Show *me your ways, O* L ORD, *teach me your paths; guide me in your truth and teach me, for you are God my Savior, and my hope is in you all day long.* —Psalm 25:4–5, emphasis mine

_____

_____

_____

_____

_____

_____DAY TWO

In bringing me to an understanding of this dilemma, the starting place had to be the sovereignty of God. Scripture is clear that God is, has always been, and will always be sovereign. Sovereign is sovereign—any limitations on His sovereignty would mean that He is not sovereign.

To say that God is sovereign is to say that He is under no rule or authority outside Himself. His sovereignty is combined with His all-powerfulness. He not only has all authority, He has all power.

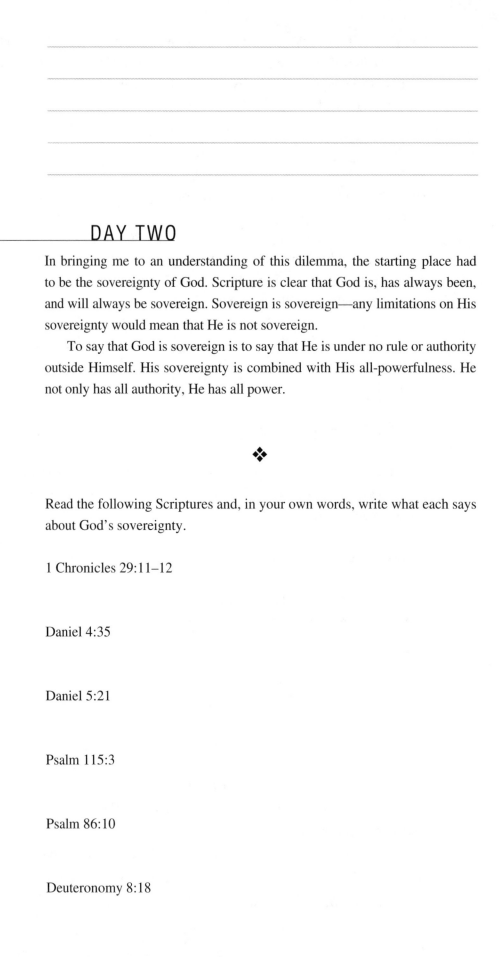

Read the following Scriptures and, in your own words, write what each says about God's sovereignty.

1 Chronicles 29:11–12

Daniel 4:35

Daniel 5:21

Psalm 115:3

Psalm 86:10

Deuteronomy 8:18

John 3:27

Proverbs 16:4

Romans 9:17

John 6:37

John 19:11

Job 42:2

Write out your understanding of the sovereignty of God.

❖

Week 1, Day 2

PRACTICE A NEW WAY OF PRAYING

What is God saying to you?

*Show **me** your ways, O LORD, teach me your paths; guide me in your truth and teach me, for you are God my Savior, and my hope is in you all day long.* —Psalm 25:4–5, emphasis mine

_____

_____

_____

_____

_____

_____

Does God change His mind? Does He ever rethink His position or second-guess His decree? Let's look at the clear words of Scripture:

God is not a man, that he should lie, nor a son of man, that he should change his mind. Does he speak and then not act? Does he promise and not fulfill? —Numbers 23:19

He who is the Glory of Israel does not lie or change his mind; for he is not a man, that he should change his mind. —1 Samuel 15:29

But the plans of the LORD stand firm forever, the purposes of his heart through all generations. —Psalm 33:11

Your word, O LORD, is eternal; it stands firm in the heavens. —Psalm 119:89

I know that everything God does will endure forever; nothing can be added to it and nothing taken from it. God does it so that men will revere him. —Ecclesiastes 3:14

Consider what God has done: Who can straighten what he has made crooked? —Ecclesiastes 7:13

For God's gifts and his call are irrevocable. —Romans 11:29

He does not take back his words. —Isaiah 31:2

The Word of God, from beginning to end, tells us that God is sovereign and that He is working according to a plan that has been in place since before the earth was formed. Nothing takes Him by surprise. He is never making things up as He goes along. He is never confronted with a situation He had not expected and planned for and woven into His sovereign and redemptive plan. As Isaiah stated, He does not take back His words.

Yet there are occasions in Scripture when it appears that God changed His mind in response to intercession. For example, in the story recorded in Exodus 32:9–14, the Israelites angered God by building a golden calf to worship. God declared that as a result of their idolatry, He would destroy them and make a great nation out of Moses. But Moses began to pray: "*Turn from your fierce anger; relent* (change your mind) *and do not bring disaster on your people*" (Exodus 32:12, parentheses added). How does the Scripture say that God responded to Moses' prayer? "*Then the LORD relented and did not bring on His people the disaster He had threatened*" (Exodus 32:14).

How can we reconcile the sovereign and unchangeable purposes of God with the intercession of His people? The question of God's sovereignty and man's will—both clearly taught in Scripture—continue to confuse many. Since both are taught in Scripture, both are fully true and they are fully true *at the same time*. See the appendixes of this book for a fuller treatment of this issue.

Did God change His mind? Let's set this passage into its context—the whole Word of God and all of history. The story is told from the earth's point of view. But you and I are not limited to the earth's point of view. We can see it from heaven's point of view. We can step back and get the big picture. From the earth, it looked as if Moses prayed and God changed His mind. But is that what really happened?

If God changed His mind in response to Moses' prayer, then was Moses more merciful than God? Was Moses wiser than God? Did Moses get God to cool His anger so that He wouldn't take an action He would ultimately regret? Shall we be grateful to Moses for restraining God?

Or is this the way it happened? God sees the sin of the nation of Israel and passes judgment on them—they will be destroyed. But Moses makes such a passionate plea on their behalf that God reevaluates. "Moses has a point," He reasons. "I hadn't thought about it that way. I'll change My mind and do as Moses has suggested."

Was it Moses? Was it Moses' character and persuasiveness that influenced God? If so, then Moses' prayers should always have been answered affirmatively, but they were not. In the instance reported by Moses in Deuteronomy 3:26, Moses says, *"But because of you the Lord was angry with me, and would not listen to me. 'That is enough,' the Lord said. 'Do not speak to me anymore about this matter.'"* Moses had tried to change God's mind about letting him enter the Promised Land, but he could not. The answer to this dilemma does not lie in Moses and his ability to pray well.

Is this not a true statement? If God can be influenced to change His mind, then His word cannot be trusted. Think about it. If the right argument can change God's mind, then how can His word stand firm in the heavens (Psalm 119:89)? How can His word endure when all else fades like the grass of the field (Isaiah 40:8)?

Think about it. If the right argument can change God's mind, then how can His word stand firm in the heavens? How can His word endure when all else fades like the grass of the field?

Write out your answers to these questions. For now, just answer with a simple yes or no. We'll continue to think through the whole issue.

Was Moses wiser and more merciful than God?

Did God re-think His position?

Did God surrender His sovereignty to Moses?

Did Moses change God's mind?

Week 1, Day 3

PRACTICE A NEW WAY OF PRAYING

What is God saying to you?

*Show me **your ways**, O LORD, teach me your paths; guide me in your truth and teach me, for you are God my Savior, and my hope is in you all day long.* —Psalm 25:4–5, emphasis mine

----

DAY FOUR

We begin to see the truth when we compare two similar events that have different outcomes. One is found in Exodus 32, the passage we looked at yesterday. The other is found in Ezekiel 22.

Read Ezekiel 22:23–31 and answer the following questions:

Why was the nation of Judah in danger of receiving God's judgment?

What did God do "*so* [He] *would not have to destroy it* (Judah)?"

Examine the two situations side by side and you will see a parallel spiritual truth running through them. Notice the similarities in the two situations:

In both instances, the people had broken covenant with God.

Read Exodus 32:1–6. Israel broke covenant with God. Then read Ezekiel 22:23–29. Judah broke covenant with God.

In both instances, the people had earned God's judgment.

What is God's judgment? It is when God allows the consequences of sin to accruc to the sinner. God does not *impose* a new punishment for each offense. I am not saying that God does not punish. I am saying that sin has punishment built into it. When God defined judgment or punishment to Adam and Eve, He did not say, "If you eat of the tree of the knowledge of good and evil, I will kill you." He said, *"You will die."* The wages of sin is death. Sin brings death and punishment with it.

God's judgment occurs when God allows sin to have its full effect and does not intervene to circumvent the evil. Notice what God said about His actions toward Judah in Ezekiel 22:31: *"bringing down on their own heads all they have done."*

In both instances, God desired to intervene in the natural course of events and show mercy instead of judgment.

For the nation of Israel in Exodus 32, we know that God's heart desire was not to destroy the people, but to save them. How do we know? Look at the judgment the people had earned. God said to Moses, *"I will destroy this nation and make a great nation out of you."* Think about it. What if God had carried out the judgment? He would have destroyed the tribe that was to produce the Messiah! The Messiah was to come from the tribe of Judah, but Moses was from the tribe of Levi. God did not want judgment; He wanted to show mercy.

For the nation of Judah in Ezekiel 22, we know that God wanted to show mercy because He said, *"I looked for a man among them who would build up the wall and stand before me in the gap on behalf of the land so I would not have to destroy it."*

In both cases, even though the people had earned judgment, God desired mercy.

When God wanted to intervene and change the natural course of events, what did He do? In both instances, He looked for an intercessor.

Read Exodus 32:7–10, God's call to Moses. Look at the elements of the call:

1. **Verse 7**: God reminds Moses that He has placed the people into Moses' care. When He called the nation of Israel "*your people, whom you brought up out of Egypt*" instead of "*My people, whom I brought up out of Egypt*," what was He meaning to communicate? He was saying to Moses, "Moses, My people, whom I have entrusted to your care..."

2. **Verses 8–10**: God tells Moses what the people have brought on themselves. He gives Moses a glimpse of where things are headed unless God intervenes. Isn't that what motivates us to intercede? Don't we first have to see the urgency? God called forth from Moses the great love for the people that God Himself had placed in Moses' heart.

3. **Verse 10b**: God said to Moses, "I will destroy them. Then I will make you into a great nation." We have to hear this statement in the context of the relationship between God and Moses. God and Moses had lived in such long intimacy that the heart of God had become the heart of Moses. The desires of God had become the desires of Moses. Moses did not see a good opportunity to exalt himself, but instead saw the destruction of God's eternal plan. God called on Moses' selfless love for the people and his loyalty to the eternal purposes of God. With these words, God called Moses into intercession.

Read Ezekiel 22:30. What does God clearly state? "*I looked for a man*." God looked for an intercessor for Judah.

Now the two instances take opposite turns.

When God looked for an intercessor for Israel, He found Moses.

When God looked for an intercessor for Judah, He found no one.

Israel received mercy. Judah received judgment.

Israel: Exodus 32	Judah: Ezekiel 22
Israel breaks covenant with God. (Exodus 32:1–4)	Judah breaks covenant with God. (Ezekiel 22:23–29)
Israel deserves judgment. (Exodus 32:8)	Judah deserves judgment. (Ezekiel 22:30)
God desires mercy. (Genesis 49:10—God wants to preserve Messiah's tribe)	God desires mercy. (Ezekiel 22:30)
God seeks out an intercessor. (Exodus 32:7–10)	God looks for an intercessor. (Ezekiel 22:30)
God finds Moses. (Exodus 32:11)	God finds no one. (Ezekiel 22:30)
Israel receives mercy. (Exodus 32:14)	Judah receives judgment. (Ezekiel 22:31)

Moses did not change God's mind; He shared God's mind. He did not alter God's plan; He implemented God's plan. God's purposes were firmly rooted in Moses' heart and formed the basis for Moses' desires. When Moses spontaneously poured out his heart to God, God's desires were being expressed through Moses' lips. From a one-dimensional, earth-based point of view, it appeared that Moses had changed God's mind. Instead, through his intercession, Moses reflected God's love and redemptive purposes.

What God wants to do on the earth, He will do through intercessors. Prayer releases the will of God, bringing His will out of the spiritual realm and causing it to take effect in the material realm. Prayer opens the way for God to do what He longs to do. When God wants to change the course events will take on their own, He calls out an intercessor.

When God found no intercessor for Judah, the people suffered the full consequences of their actions. The different outcomes, mercy as opposed to judgment, hinged on the availability of an intercessor.

Two questions arise: (1) What if Moses had not been available to intercede? Would God's eternal plan have been thwarted? If that's the case, doesn't God's sovereignty hinge on man's obedience? (2) If God wanted to show mercy to Judah, but did not because there was no one to intercede, was God's sovereignty not limited by man's disobedience? To explore these questions, see the appendixes *Man's Will/God's Sovereignty* and *Is God's Sovereignty Limited to Man's Obedience?* found in the back of this book.

Prayer does not change God, but prayer does change the circumstances of earth. If we approach prayer as if God's mind needed to be changed, then aren't we starting out with the supposition that God is about to make a mistake? But if we understand that every thought and intention in the mind of God is good and righteous, then we will enthusiastically cooperate with Him, praying His power and provision onto the earth.

Note: There are several instances in Scripture when it appears that God changed His mind. To explore those in detail, see the article *Does God Change His Mind?* found in the appendixes of this book.

Did Moses change God's mind?

a. Yes. God was swayed by Moses' reasoning and passion and decided to take Moses' suggestion.

b. No. When Moses poured out his own deep desires, He was expressing the heart and mind of God.

What God wants to do on the earth, He will do through intercessors. When God wants to intervene and change the course events will take on their own, He searches out an intercessor upon whose heart He can place His own desires.

What is your reaction to the statement above?
I agree because:

I disagree because:

Week 1, Day 4

PRACTICE A NEW WAY OF PRAYING

What is God saying to you?

*Show me your ways, O LORD, **teach me** your paths; **guide me** in your truth and teach me, for you are God my Savior, and my hope is in you all day long.* —Psalm 25:4–5, emphasis mine

DAY FIVE

Continue to look at Moses' praying life. How did it operate? What did his prayers accomplish?

One thing that you will learn in this course is that prayer is more than the words that come sandwiched between "Dear God" and "Amen." Prayer is an ongoing interaction between the material world and the spiritual world. It takes many forms. One of those forms is active, aggressive obedience to God's revealed will. Look at Moses' praying life when he led the Israelites out of Egypt and found himself caught between the Egyptian army and the Red Sea.

Read Exodus 14:15–18 and think through these questions:
When Moses found himself in this difficulty, was it a surprise to God?

Did God passively allow the situation, or did He actively engineer it? (Read Exodus 14:1–4.) What was His purpose?

Before Moses and the Israelites arrived at the Red Sea, did God already know what He was going to do to save them?

Did God do what He planned to do and wanted to do without Moses' active participation? Read Exodus 14:16 and 21–22.

When Moses found himself in this difficult situation, what was his role?
  a. To figure out how God could rescue them and suggest it to Him.
  b. To talk God into rescuing them.
  c. To figure out a way to get the people to the other side of the sea, where God wanted them.
  d. To respond in obedience to God's voice and let his praying life be the conduit to bring into the situation what God had always planned to do.

What is God's intent for prayer? The purpose of prayer is **to release the power of God to accomplish the purposes of God.** The purpose of prayer is to discover God's will, not obligate Him to do mine; to reflect God's mind, not change it. I could, through prayer, release God's power to bring about the best possible solution in every situation, because that is always God's desire. "'*For I know the plans I have for you,' declares the* LORD, *'plans to prosper you and not to harm you, plans to give you hope and a future*'" (Jeremiah 29:11). Could I learn, like Moses, to make my heart available for God's purposes? Could I learn to trust His purposes more than my own perceptions?

My first step, finding a new purpose for prayer, would require an inner transformation. Changing my prayer focus from my own satisfaction and happiness to God's glory and eternal purposes would take a brand new heart. God has promised just such a drastic reorientation: "*I will give you a new heart and put a new spirit in you; I will remove from you your heart of stone and give you a heart of flesh. And I will put my Spirit in you and move you to follow my decrees and be careful to keep my laws*" (Ezekiel 36:26–27). Before I desired such a thing, God had made it available. He had already promised to reproduce His heart in me, shaping my desires to match His. He promised to take my self-centered heart and fasten it on Him. And He worked in me until I desired to receive what He desired to give. "*It is God who works in you to will…his good purpose*" (Philippians 2:13).

Think about the following passage from one of my books, *Heart's Cry: Principles of Prayer.*

And we, who with unveiled faces all reflect the Lord's glory, are being transformed into his likeness with ever-increasing glory, which comes from the Lord, who is the Spirit. —**2 Corinthians 3:18**

As you behold His glory, you are changed so that your heart is a reflection of His. His concerns are your concerns. His desires are your desires. His will is reflected in your prayers. In His presence, your prayer life becomes consistently powerful and effective. This is not because you now have more influence on Him, but because He now has more influence on you. The secret of prayer is not how to change God, but how to be changed by Him.

Could I learn, like Moses, to make my heart available for God's purposes? Could I learn to trust His purposes more than my own perceptions?

Week 1, Day 5

PRACTICE A NEW WAY OF PRAYING

What is God saying to you?

Show me your ways, O LORD, teach me **your paths***; guide me in* **your truth** *and teach me, for you are God my Savior, and my hope is in you all day long.* —Psalm 25:4–5, emphasis mine

_____

_____

_____

_____

_____

Week One Anniversary Thought

The first breakthrough understanding about prayer is that there is no recipe to follow, no "ten easy steps" to power in prayer. Power praying does not require that you master a skill, but that you pursue a present-tense relationship with the living and indwelling Jesus.

Prayer marked Jesus' life. Long, extended times of prayer. Spontaneous eruptions of prayer. Prayer in public, and with His disciples. Certainly Jesus, who only did and spoke what the Father showed Him, did not use prayer to argue, or beg, or try to change God's mind. Then why did Jesus pray? Why was prayer such a hallmark of His life that His disciples asked Him to teach them to pray like He prayed? If He wasn't giving God instructions, what was He doing when He rose up early to pray or spent all night in prayer?

I think we might get a hint from His time in Gethsemane, where some of His words are recorded and so we get a glimpse into the tenor of His interchange with the Father. We see Him synchronizing His heart with the Father's heart.

I think it works like this: I have many mobile electronic devices that I use to accomplish my daily tasks, or to entertain myself, or to stay in touch with others. I do most of my work on my main desktop computer, but then I need to transfer the work I've done, or the information I've added, or the files I've edited from my main computer to my mobile devices. How do I accomplish that? How do I get what is on the hard drive of my computer downloaded onto my mobile devices? I link the mobile device to the computer and a program is activated that automatically syncs my mobile device to my computer. What is on my computer is reproduced on my mobile device.

In His all-night prayer in Gethsemane, we see Jesus linking His heart to the Father's. Let me summarize the content of His recorded prayer in some new words. "Father, download Your will into my heart so that it overwrites any other desire. Download courageous faith that deletes fear. Synchronize My heart's desire to Yours."

What came from that heart-to-heart transaction? Observe the Jesus who emerges from His hours of agony. Courageous, forceful, marching out to meet His enemy rather than waiting to be taken. Handing Himself over to the purposes of the Father without reservation.

"The hour has come. Look, the Son of Man is betrayed into the hands of sinners. Rise! Let us go! Here comes my betrayer!" (Mark 14:41–42).

The Definition of Prayer

PRACTICE A NEW WAY OF PRAYING

This week, take the Scripture for the day and pray it. Put the words of the promise into the form of a petition. Make your Scripture-prayer specific to your life and situation. This is how you harvest His ripe and ready promises. Thank God for watching over His Word to see that it is carried out. (See Jeremiah 1:12.)

DAY ONE

To bring my prayers into alignment with His purposes, I had to redefine prayer completely. If prayer is not for the purpose of moving God to my point of view, what is prayer? If I can't change God, why should I pray?

A new definition of prayer began to emerge in my life and thinking. Prayer is not a group of words sandwiched between "Dear God" and "Amen." It is not begging, pleading, convincing, or twisting God's arm. Prayer is not a way to get God to do what we want Him to do when we want Him to do it. I had been telling God what to do, expressed in religious-sounding words, and expecting Him to obey me. When He didn't obey me, I was disappointed in Him. Prayer, I learned, is not expecting God to carry out my decisions. Prayer is not giving God instructions to follow.

"To pray is to let Jesus glorify His name in the midst of our needs," says O. Hallesby in his book, *Prayer*. Prayer is simply opening our lives to God, acknowledging our total dependence on Him. Prayer is not limited to a segment of our lives or to a scheduled event in our days. It is an attitude of receptivity in which we live every moment. It is being open to Him at all times. It is living in the presence of God, always in the process of being reshaped and recreated by Him.

Finish the following thought: Prayer is

a. the way to get things from God.

b. the way to bring your needs to God's attention.

c. like a phone line between me and God. God is not paying attention until He hears me say, "Dear God."

d. none of the above.

❖

PRACTICE A NEW WAY OF PRAYING

Turn this promise into a prayer.

"For I know the plans I have for you," declares the LORD, "plans to prosper you and not to harm you, plans to give you hope and a future."
—Jeremiah 29:11

_____

_____

_____

_____

_____

DAY TWO

Misconceptions about prayer limit us. These misunderstandings are perhaps not articulated, but they are obvious in our approach to prayer and our expectations about prayer. The truth about prayer will free us to pray with the boldness God intends.

Misconception #1: Prayer is only for material needs. Some pray as if prayer is the way to get things from God. Does God tell us to ask Him for the material things we need? Yes, He does. Is it wrong to ask God for material things? No, God encourages it. However, this is not the primary purpose for prayer. If your prayer life is limited to placing your orders with God and expecting Him to fulfill them in a timely manner, I imagine you have often been disappointed.

Prayer for material needs is presented by Jesus as the very simplest kind of prayer. This kind of prayer requires the least amount of spiritual energy. Jesus teaches, first of all, that your Father knows what you need before you ask Him (Matthew 6:8). Then He goes on to tell His followers that they do not have to worry about what to eat or what to wear. He points us to nature and the splendor with which the Father clothes the lilies of the field and the care with which He watches the birds of the air. He says, speaking of material things, "Your Father knows that you need them." You do not have to convince Him of your need. Not only does He know your need, He also cares about your need. You are more important to Him than the birds and the lilies. His provision for them is ample evidence that He will provide for you. You do not have to persevere and struggle in prayer for material needs. Since that's the case, you can focus on seeking His kingdom and His righteousness, certain that your needs will be met (Matthew 6:25–34). Jesus said, "*I tell you the truth, unless you change and become like little children, you will never enter the kingdom of heaven*" (Matthew 18:3). To see the kingdom of God clearly, one must leave behind adult pretenses and sophisticated arguments. Often, we come to God prepared to do battle with Him, convince Him of the validity of our need, and give Him reasons to meet it.

What a contrast to the way a little child comes to his or her parents! A child simply assumes that the need or desire is potent enough to speak for itself. All that is required is to bring that need to Mom's or Dad's attention. The request assumes the answer. The child's only thought is to bring the need to the source of supply.

You don't need to build a theological case for why God should want to meet your need. He wants to meet your need because He's your daddy and you are the apple of His eye. Jesus highlights the simplicity of supplication by saying, "*Ask and it will be given to you.... For everyone who asks receives*" (Matthew 7:7–8). The Greek word translated *ask* is used to ask for something to be given, not done. It is the simplest, most straightforward picture of asking for something you need.

But when a person seeks to use prayer merely as a means of obtaining material things, either needs or desire, that person will never discover the overwhelming and awe-inspiring power available through prayer. It is very simple for God to supply your material needs, and He does so willingly.

Misconception #2: Prayer is to convince God to implement our ideas. Some pray as if prayer will give God new information or inspire Him to new ideas. Some approach prayer as if it is the responsibility of the petitioner to decide what God needs to do and then talk Him into doing it. This kind of pray-er sees himself as constantly having to overcome God's objections, or His inertia, or His procrastination. This person feels that God always starts out against him and must be won over. Prayer of this kind pits the pray-er against God. It feels like a battle of wills.

You don't need to build a theological case for why God should want to meet your need. He wants to meet your need because He's your daddy and you are the apple of His eye.

As with every misconception about prayer, this error causes the praying person to expend spiritual energy needlessly. The person who prays in this way tends to look for the right formula, or the right words to say, or the right order in which to say them. This person is always on a quest to find the approach to God that will finally get Him to act.

This person believes the myth that it is hard to get God to answer prayer. The truth is that God longs to do His work on earth in response to prayer. Prayer is His idea. God thought up prayer, not humans.

God answers prayer, but He doesn't follow instructions. God corrects those who attempt to instruct Him. "*Who has understood the mind of the LORD, or instructed him as his counselor? Whom did the LORD consult to enlighten him, and who taught him the right way? Who was it that taught him knowledge or showed him the path of understanding?*" (Isaiah 40:13–14). However, God loves our prayers. He rejoices in them. They bring Him pleasure. They are a sweet-smelling aroma to Him (Revelation 5:8; Psalm 141:2).

Power praying happens when God, who longs to give, is met by man, who longs to receive. God is the initiator. He made promises and invited petition. The secret to power praying lies not in how to ask, but in how to receive.

Misconception #3: Prayer is to hold God to His promises. Some pray as if God forgets or tries to renege on His promises and is depending on pray-ers to remind Him of them. God does not need to be reminded of His promises. He made promises and bound Himself to us in a blood-sealed covenant so that we would know exactly what we could expect from Him. God made promises to us in order to stir up hope and expectation so that we would have reason to turn to Him. The purpose of His promises is to give us confidence and peace. Instead, sometimes we pray as if we are responsible for finding the scriptural promise that can be construed as guaranteeing the outcome we have prescribed, then taking that promise to God to hold Him to His Word.

This kind of pray-er treats God's Word as if it were a catalog. He decides what God should do, looks through the Bible to find a verse that will match that plan, and orders it. In doing so, as in catalog shopping, the pray-er skims over everything that holds no appeal. He picks and chooses.

Remember, Scripture is not God's words; it is God's *Word*. Scripture is a whole and cannot be cut apart and pasted together to match my agenda. His Word is not a catalog. It is His promise in writing.

When we approach prayer this way—as if God might try to get out of meeting our need, but since we have His promise, we can hold Him to it—we become drained of energy and suffer from prayer fatigue. What a burden it is for me to search the Scripture and find exactly the right verse to bring to God's attention. Instead, as I turn my heart and my mind toward Him, He reminds *me* of His promises. He reminds me of what I can count on. The promises are not for me to use in getting my way with God, but they are for God to use to inspire faith and confidence within me.

Misconception #4: Prayer helps pry riches out of God's reluctant hands. Some pray as if prayer is the means of cajoling God into releasing His carefully hoarded riches. Someone has said, "Prayer is not overcoming God's reluctance, but laying hold of God's willingness." God offers us His resources. He invites us to take His gifts. He does not have to be convinced to let go of His blessings. His Word says that He lavishes on us the riches of His grace (Ephesians 1:7–8) and that He lavishes His love on us (1 John 3:1). He is extravagant in His gifts. He pours them out. Scripture never uses language that would portray God as stingy or hesitant to give. Instead we read that He "richly blesses all who call on him" (Romans 10:12).

When we pray this way, we expend spiritual energy needlessly trying to convince God of something He already knows. Giving you every good thing gives Him joy; it delights Him. Jesus assures us with these words: *"Do not be afraid, little flock, for your Father has been pleased to give you the kingdom"* (Luke 12:32). His heart is set on you to do you good.

The Truth About Prayer

The truth about prayer will set you free. Prayer is the means by which you will be freed from your earthbound, timebound thinking to participate in eternity. True prayer releases His power so that His power can accomplish immeasurably more than we can ask or even imagine (Ephesians 3:20).

The truth about prayer will set you free.

God's power—the power released by prayer—is power that has a direct and observable impact on the earth. Paul describes the power available through prayer in Ephesians 1:19–20: *"His incomparably great power for us who believe. That power is like the working of his mighty strength, which he exerted in Christ when he raised him from the dead and seated him at his right hand in the heavenly realms."*

God's power, which is beyond comparison, is available to "us who believe." The same power that put eternal life into the dead body of Jesus, the same power that lifted Jesus above all other rule and authority, that same power—"the working of his mighty strength"—is released into the material realm when we pray.

God means for prayer always to bring His power to earth. His intent is that every prayer find His "yes." *"For the Son of God, Jesus Christ…was not 'Yes' and 'No,' but in him it has always been 'Yes.' For no matter how many promises God has made, they are 'Yes' in Christ"* (2 Corinthians 1:19–20).

Prayer will work as God intends for it to work when it becomes what God intends for it to be. Prayer is not an activity, but a relationship. Prayer is not a formula, but a life. Only when we have learned how to live prayer, breathe prayer, be prayer—only then will the power available through prayer be consistently manifested on the earth. God has ordained that prayer will be the conduit through which His intervening, earth-changing power flows from heaven to earth. Prayer is what sets God's will in motion on the earth.

Which misconception(s) do you see in your own prayer life?

Do you believe that it is hard to get God to answer prayer?

In praying, do you find yourself pleading with God or begging God?

What styles of communication worked when you were trying to get something from your parents? Do you find yourself trying to use those same methods on God?

Week 2, Day 2
PRACTICE A NEW WAY OF PRAYING

Turn this promise into a prayer.

"'I will give you a new heart and put a new spirit in you....And I will put my Spirit in you and move you to follow my decrees and be careful to keep my laws.'" —Ezekiel 36:26–27

DAY THREE

Peter writes that we are *"partakers of the divine nature"* (2 Peter 1:4 NASB). Think about that statement. We *take part in* the divine nature. The divine nature becomes available to us. Do you see how rich that phrase is? God, who is Spirit, imparts Himself to us. It is through the ongoing and increasingly intimate communion with Him that our participation in the divine nature becomes solid and real. Through prayer, He is reproducing His heart in us.

"Prayer…is the means whereby we assimilate more and more of His mind," writes Oswald Chambers in his book, *Christian Disciplines.* Watchman Nee states it this way: "Prayer is the union of the believer's thought with the will of God. The prayer which a believer utters on earth is but the voicing of the Lord's will in heaven."

The key to powerful praying is learning how to let Him pour His own desires into my heart and make them mine. In every circumstance, the Holy Spirit, who knows the mind of God, will teach us to pray as we ought, will shape our prayers, will pray through us. Little by little, under His loving tutelage, we will find our prayers reflecting God's will.

What do you think is the key to assimilating the mind and heart of God?

What do you think are barriers in your life to assimilating the mind and heart of God?

Week 2, Day 3

PRACTICE A NEW WAY OF PRAYING

Turn this promise into a prayer.

"May you be richly rewarded by the LORD, the God of Israel, under whose wings you have come to take refuge." —Ruth 2:12

DAY FOUR

While discovering the true purpose of prayer, and while redefining what prayer is, we must also learn to give up our tendency to see God's will as if it could be fully defined within the context of one circumstance; as if God's will in each circumstance stood alone. God is working out His will according to an eternal strategy. Each individual piece will be part of the big plan.

Suppose that I handed you one piece of a 5,000-piece jigsaw puzzle. Imagine that I asked you to look at that piece and tell me what the whole puzzle looks like. You couldn't possibly do it. Standing alone, the puzzle piece seems random and without purpose. Only when it's placed in its proper context does it begin to make sense. So it is with life. Each circumstance fits into the big picture. Don't waste your time trying to make each piece make sense by itself. We tend to try to define God's will incident by incident, happening by happening, as if each occurrence in our lives stands alone. Instead, everything is being blended together into the whole. "*The LORD works out everything for his own ends*" (Proverbs 16:4).

God's work in our lives in response to prayer is an ongoing eternal design instead of many isolated plans. God's will flows through circumstances. His work in one circumstance sets the stage for the next. Over the course of time, there will be circumstances that, although you have prayed, seem not to have worked out according to God's revealed will. But wait! Watch to see what God does next. Watch to see which element of your disappointing circumstance is the catalyst for the next victory. Watch how the immediate flows into the ultimate.

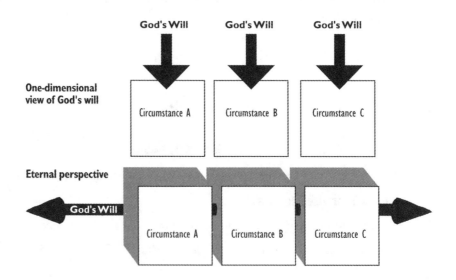

Don't focus your faith on a specific outcome; focus your faith on God. Jesus' instruction is, "*Have faith in God*" (Mark 11:22). When you place your faith in an outcome, you will often be disappointed. When you put your faith in God, you will never be disappointed.

For example, suppose that you said to me, "Will you pray that God will give me a car so that I can get to work?" My response to you would be, "I won't pray that God will give you a car, but I will pray that God will get you to work." Perhaps God wants to provide you with a ride with someone who will open the door for the next step in His plan. If your prayer focus is a car, but God provides for your need in another way, you will think that God has said no to your prayer. It will go in your "unanswered prayers" category.

When you are in a situation that has an outcome that seems not to be according to God's will, wait to see what happens next. The story is not over. That circumstance will set the stage for the next event, which will lay the foundation for the next step, which will open the door for the next piece of the plan, and on and on. Finally, you will look back from a place in your life that is *"immeasurably more than all [you] ask or imagine"* (Ephesians 3:20), and you will say, "I could not be *here* if I'd never been *there*."

As God's power and provision flow through your life, blending one circumstance into the next, you will find that the story is never over. Don't put a period where God has put a comma. There is no end. What looks like a defeat is the ground from which victory will grow. What looks like the end is really the beginning. A crucifixion is only the prelude to a resurrection. Consider Jesus' lifeless body bound in graveclothes, laid in the tomb. It looked to His followers like the end.

The tomb.
Place of death.
Full of dark night
And suffocating hopelessness.
The end.

Became the Beginning
And the womb from which
Eternal Life emerged.

Have you ever been disappointed in God? Have you ever felt that God let you down? Write out a memory of a time when you felt that God did not come through for you.

Look back at that incident with the perspective that time brings. What were you expecting of God? Is the issue that He did not do what you expected Him to do? Can you now go back to that disappointment and trace God's hand? What did God's unexpected action—the action that disappointed you—open the way for? What did God do through your circumstance that He could have done no other way?

What is a circumstance in your life about which you are concerned and praying?

What is it that you think God should do? How do you think He should resolve it? Write out your thoughts in detail.

Are you focusing your faith on the outcome that you have prescribed? Or is your faith in God? Can you give up your instructions to God and ask Him to do His will in His way at His time?

❖

Week 2, Day 4

PRACTICE A NEW WAY OF PRAYING

Turn this promise into a prayer.

Many are the plans in a man's heart, but it is the LORD's purpose that prevails. —Proverbs 19:21

_____

_____

_____

_____

_____

_____

DAY FIVE

If a praying life is a life open to God, and if we begin to live with our spiritual senses alert to the spiritual realm, it will require a fully devoted heart. Do you wonder how you will find the time for such total devotion? Does it sound as if God is calling upon you to live a cloistered life, oblivious to the many practical demands of day-to-day living? A praying life requires no such thing! With the Holy Spirit as your guide, you will discover a deeper level of living and responding. You are always involved in thinking and feeling, aren't you? You will learn to make God the focal point of your unceasing thought processes and find yourself involved in unceasing prayer. It will become your soul's habit to turn every thought toward God.

Your mind is an amazing creation. It functions efficiently on many levels at once. It is the ultimate multitasking software. At one time you may be driving a car, remembering directions, carrying on a conversation, retaining a grocery list in your memory, observing the time, and on and on and on. There are mental processes going on that you are not even aware of. Consider this: At one of those levels, prayer is always going on. This is true because the Spirit of Christ lives in you and He is always praying. Sometimes, prayer is at the most conscious and aware level of thought. Other times it is down a level or two. Once I realized that, it became easier and more natural for me to switch back and forth—to bring prayer back to the higher awareness level more often and more spontaneously. The reason is that I don't always feel like I'm starting over. I realize that I'm in a continuous flow of prayer. I didn't stop praying, start doing something else, then start praying all over again. The sweet aroma of prayer is always rising from your innermost being before the throne.

Psalm 139:4 says, "*Before a word is on my tongue you know it completely, O Lord.*" Before a need or desire has reached a level of conscious understanding at which you can put it into words—while it is still unformed and raw—God already knows it fully. In Romans 8:26–27, we read, "*The Spirit himself intercedes for us with groans that words cannot express. And he who searches our hearts knows the mind of the Spirit, because the Spirit intercedes for the saints in accordance with God's will.*" When a desire is nothing but an inarticulate groan—before you can form it into sentences— the Spirit of God is already speaking it with perfect clarity. By the time you begin to speak your need or desire in prayer, you are simply joining into a flow of prayer that is already in progress. "*Before they call I will answer; while they are still speaking I will hear*" (Isaiah 65:24).

What do you think Paul means when he says, "*Pray without ceasing*"? (See 1 Thessalonians 5:17 NASB).

Have you ever felt inadequate in the face of that command? Why or why not?

Write down how your concept of unceasing prayer has expanded. What will this new understanding mean to you?

Week 2, Day 5

PRACTICE A NEW WAY OF PRAYING

Turn this promise into a prayer.

Who, then, is the man that fears the LORD? He will instruct him in the way chosen for him. —Psalm 25:12

_____

_____

_____

_____

_____

Week Two Anniversary Thought

A praying life requires a 180-degree about-face from the direction our human nature would lead us. Our flesh is bent on doing a good job, getting it right, proving our ability. A praying life is built on a principle that is the polar opposite of our flesh's instincts: letting go, yielding, admitting helplessness. It doesn't come easily to us.

Jesus ratified this principle as of primary importance in His first formal sermon. We refer to His opening remarks as the Beatitudes. The first words out of Jesus' mouth, once the crowd had gathered, were *"Blessed are the poor in spirit, for theirs is the kingdom of heaven"* (Matthew 5:3). Prayer is reaching into the kingdom and drawing on its resources. What is the prerequisite for having complete access to the kingdom? Being poor in spirit.

The word for "poor" means destitute: a beggar whose only hope is to receive from the hand of another. Until we recognize the blessedness of being wholly dependent on God, who even produces prayer in us, we won't live in the abundance that could be ours. Our helplessness is our strongest plea. I illustrated this concept in *Set Apart* as follows:

I recently had the tiniest glimpse of how powerfully helplessness speaks. A few years ago, I lost my husband to brain cancer. During the final months of his illness, he became utterly helpless. The man I had leaned on for 25 years, whose strength I counted on, was now dependent upon me for his every need. During those weeks, my ear was tuned to his every sigh, his every restless movement, every change in his breathing pattern. If I had to be out of his room for even a few minutes, I had a monitor with me so I could hear him if he needed me. When he was strong, I was not so attentive. His needs did not fill my waking moments, when he could meet them himself. His helplessness spoke louder than any word he might have spoken. Because of his helplessness—because I knew he could do nothing on his own—I was on watch day and night.

My experience is but a pale shadow of the reality of the Kingdom, but still it helps me understand how my weakness is the opening for His strength. The fact of my helplessness is the only prayer I need. It speaks louder than eloquence.

Your helplessness is your best prayer. It calls from your heart to the heart of God with greater effect than all your uttered pleas. He hears it from the very moment that you are seized with helplessness, and He becomes actively engaged at once in hearing and answering the prayer of your helplessness.
—Ole Hallesby,
Prayer

The Necessity of Prayer

DAY ONE

Although prayer does not change God's will, it does activate God's will. Prayer releases the power of God to accomplish the will of God in situations and in the lives of people. Prayer is the channel through which God's will is brought to earth. He has a veritable flood of mercies dammed up because there is no prayer to open the floodgates. O. Hallesby says, "Prayer is the conduit through which power from heaven is brought to earth."

Do you find it as amazing as I do that Almighty God has chosen to condition the release of His intervening power on the prayers of His people? Andrew Murray says this:

God's intense longing to bless seems in some sense to be graciously limited by His dependence on the intercession that rises from earth. He seeks to rouse the spirit of intercession that He may be able to bestow His blessing on mankind. God regards intercession as the highest readiness to receive and to yield themselves wholly to the working of His almighty power.

It's not that God *can't* intervene to release His provisions without prayer; it's that He *won't*. *"You do not have, because you do not ask God"* (James 4:2). It is His sovereign decree that has established prayer as the bridge between the spiritual world—where His Word is settled forever (Psalm 89:2) and where all the promises of God are already "Yes" in Christ (2 Corinthians 1:19–20)—and the material world. Because of sin, there exists a gap between what God has prepared and is ready to release and what is happening on the earth. Prayer bridges that gap.

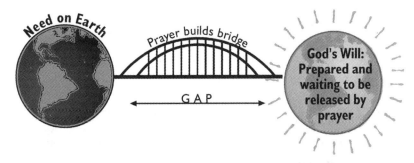

John Wesley makes this pointed statement: "God will do nothing but in answer to prayer." E. M. Bounds says, "God shapes the world by prayer." I believe that over the 13 weeks you spend in this study, you will become convinced that this is what the Scripture teaches from beginning to end: God has bound Himself to His people through prayer. It is prayer that brings God's intervening power directly to bear on situations on the earth.

If God were going to do His will without our prayers, then why did Jesus teach us to pray, "Let Your will be done on earth like Your will is done in heaven"? Jesus was showing us that our prayers release and activate God's specific will. He was teaching us a kind of praying that is aggressive and powerful. When we pray, we reach into the spiritual realm (heaven) and grab hold of the will of God for that situation. Then we pull the will of God through the gap and establish it on the earth.

"Thy kingdom come..."

Look at the following Scriptures. In each one, draw an arrow from the "cause" phrase to the "effect" phrase. The first one is an example.

"He will call upon me, and I will answer him." —Psalm 91:15

"You will seek me and find me when you seek me with all your heart." —Jeremiah 29:13

"Call to me and I will answer you and tell you great and unsearchable things you do not know." —Jeremiah 33:3

"Ask and it will be given to you; seek and you will find; knock and the door will be opened to you." —Matthew 7:7

"And I will do whatever you ask in my name, so that the Son may bring glory to the Father. You may ask me for anything in my name, and I will do it." —John 14:13–14

❖

You may be thinking, "Does this mean that God needs us? God doesn't need anyone!"

Yes, God does need us. But not because He's needy.

You and I "need" because we are needy. God needs us because He chose to. It is God, in His sovereignty, who set up the cosmos to work as He decided it should work. His sovereign decree is that His specific, intervening will in any situation will be released onto the earth by means of prayer. Prayer is the avenue that God has established for how His finished work comes from the spiritual realm and changes the earth.

Imagine that I am going to set up a corporation. I am the boss. I am sovereign over every decision about the corporation, and I have many options for how to set things up. One of the things I will decide in the beginning is this: Will I require one signature on a check or will I require two signatures on a check?

I decide that I will require two signatures. From then on, I *need* two signatures on a check. Because *I chose to need them.* Every time two signatures are required on a check, it is evidence of my sovereignty.

John the Baptist said to the Pharisees, "*I tell you that out of these stones God can raise up children for Abraham*" (Matthew 3:9). God can raise up children for Abraham out of stones. But has He ever done so? No, He has not. God can do anything He wants to do apart from His people. But the record of Scripture is clear: though He can, He, in His sovereignty, chooses not to.

Note: You may be wondering about Isaiah 59:16: "*And he saw that there was no man, and wondered that there was no intercessor: therefore his arm brought salvation unto him; and his righteousness, it sustained him*" (KJV). When you read this whole passage it will become clear that it is a messianic passage. First, it describes the hopeless condition of sin into which His people have fallen. Then it describes God anthropomorphically (describing God in human terms): He wondered, or was astonished or surprised, that there was no intercessor. Was God really shocked as you and I would be shocked? Had He really not anticipated such a situation? Then why was the Lamb slain before the foundation of the world? The "Intercessor" in this passage is the Messiah. Since there was no one capable of bridging the gap between Himself and His sinful people, He did it Himself by becoming the Kinsman-Redeemer—God made flesh. He did for us what we could not do for ourselves.

Because His power is all-sufficient, because it needs nothing to help it out or add to it, He can demonstrate His power even through jars of clay.

If you are saying, "This will lead to pride. It makes me too important in the equation!" then the full import of this has not yet hit you. When you really see this, it will be the most humbling moment of your life. When you see this, it will take your breath away.

The Almighty, the one and only, the Most High has set His heart on you. He has chosen to take you into His confidence. He has decided to condition the release of His power on the prayers of His children. Because His power is all-sufficient, because it needs nothing to help it out or add to it, He can demonstrate His power even through jars of clay.

But we have this treasure in jars of clay to show that this all-surpassing power is from God and not from us. —2 Corinthians 4:7

Power that is not diluted or undercut or diminished when it operates through fallible, silly humans—now that's **power**!

PRACTICE A NEW WAY OF PRAYING

Fix your eyes on Jesus.

_____

_____

_____

_____

_____

DAY TWO

The Bible describes prayer as "*standing in the gap*" (see Psalm 106:23 and Ezekiel 22:30). Have you ever noticed how visual the language of Scripture is? If the Bible uses a visual phrase like "stand in the gap" when He could have just said "pray," you know God has something He wants you to see. He is creating a picture of a truth to make it understandable. God is a wonderful graphic artist. He can turn an idea into a picture that speaks volumes to our visually oriented brains.

What is the picture that is painted with the phrase "stand in the gap"? First we have to answer this question: What is the gap? It seems to me that when God first created the earth, there was no gap. "*God saw all that he had made, and it was very good*" (Genesis 1:31). God, in the beginning, was pleased and satisfied with things on the earth. God's will was in effect on the earth just as His will was in effect in heaven.

Then sin entered the picture. Never again could God look at the earth and say, "That is very good." Sin created a gap between heaven and earth. Sin created a gap between what God wanted for the earth and what was happening on the earth.

Alongside the gap, place another mental picture from God's Word. God pictures His people as silver. For example, see Zechariah 13:9 and Malachi 3:3. Silver is the best conductor of power of any element on earth. Two visuals: (1) silver as a conductor and (2) a gap. Here's the whole picture. In this illustration, let the dry cell represent the power of God—ready and waiting to be released. Let the unlit light bulb represent the need on earth.

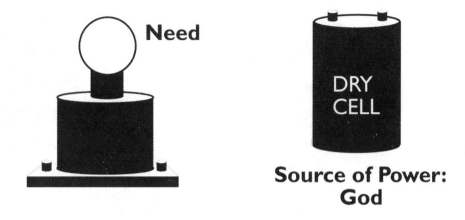

Need

Source of Power: God

The question here is simply this: how can I get the power to the need?

In the second illustration, the power and the need have been connected with a circuit. Immediately, the power begins to flow toward the need. As a picture of prayer, remember that you and I don't have to do anything to get this flow started. At His initiative, His power, His resources, His supply are flowing in our direction.

In this illustration, however, the power flow reaches a gap. When it reaches the gap, the power is not diminished or unavailable. It simply must be conducted through the gap. Electricity will not jump over the air; it requires a conductor. God's power does not jump over the gap sin has created; He requires a conductor.

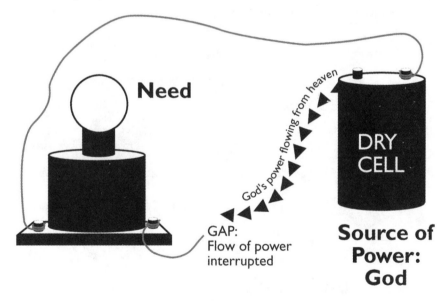

Need

God's power flowing from heaven

DRY CELL

GAP:
Flow of power
interrupted

Source of Power: God

Finally, we put all the elements together. In the following illustration, the power has begun flowing from the source to the need. This time when it reaches the gap, we insert into the gap a conductor. Look what happens— the power can flow through the gap and make its way to the need on earth.

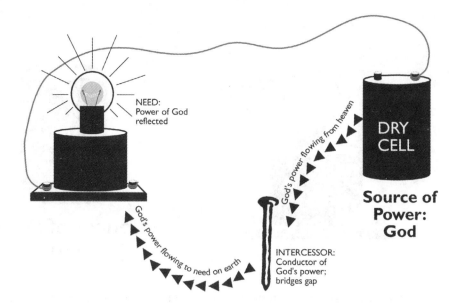

NEED:
Power of God
reflected

DRY
CELL

Source of
Power:
God

God's power flowing from heaven

God's power flowing to need on earth

INTERCESSOR:
Conductor of
God's power;
bridges gap

Prayer is standing in the gap—being the conductor of His power and His will into the circumstances on earth. It is so simple! Your prayers are the conduit that brings the power of heaven into the circumstances of earth.

When you are able to define prayer as simply conducting the will and the power of God through the gap and into the circumstances, how does it change your perspective? Think concretely—in terms of a specific need or anxiety in your life right now.

Week 3, Day 2

PRACTICE A NEW WAY OF PRAYING

Fix your eyes on Jesus.

_____

_____

_____

_____

DAY THREE

In Matthew 18:18 (NASB), Jesus says, "*Truly I say to you, whatever you bind on earth shall have been bound in heaven; and whatever you loose on earth shall have been loosed in heaven.*" The tense of the verb is crucial here. It says that the action has been fully completed in heaven before it can be bound or loosed on earth. Prayer does not change what has been done in heaven, but releases it. Whatever heaven has bound, prayer will bind on the earth. Whatever heaven has loosed, prayer will loose on the earth. Prayer causes the proclamations of heaven to be enacted on earth.

Let's look at several examples from Scripture in which it is clear that God looks for intercessors on whose hearts He can place His desires. As Andrew Murray has written, "The work of His Spirit follows the prayers of His people."

In Daniel 9, we see Daniel, who is a captive in Babylon, reading the Word of God. He reads in the Book of Jeremiah that the desolation of Jerusalem, which is the reason Daniel is in Babylon (Daniel 1:1–4), is to be in effect for 70 years. When Daniel reads this, the desolation of Jerusalem has been in effect for 70 years. "*In the first year of his reign, I, Daniel, understood from the Scriptures, according to the word of the LORD given to Jeremiah the prophet, that the desolation of Jerusalem would last seventy years*" (Daniel 9:2). Putting this verse into its historical setting, the first year of the reign of Darius, son of Xerxes, was the seventieth year of Judah's captivity.

So Daniel saw God's will and God's plan clearly revealed in the Word. What did Daniel do? Did he sit back and wait for God to do His will? No! Daniel understood that prayer is the conduit that brings God's will out of the spiritual realm and causes it to take effect on the earth. Daniel began to pray. "*So I turned to the Lord God and pleaded with him in prayer and petition, in fasting, and in sackcloth and ashes*" (Daniel 9:3). Daniel began to pray, in essence, "Let Your kingdom come and let Your will be done on earth the way You've declared it in heaven. What You have loosed in heaven, now loose on the earth." Indeed, the desolation of Jerusalem did end. In the year 538 B.C., the first year of Darius' reign, Judah began to return from exile. (See 2 Chronicles 36:20–23.)

What was the purpose of Daniel's prayer?

a. To bring the matter to God's attention. To convince God to end the captivity of Judah.

b. To influence God, or to shape God's will.

c. To release the power of God for the purposes of God.

When God reveals His will to us, how are we to respond?

Look at the next chapter of Daniel, Daniel 10. A revelation had come to Daniel, but the meaning of the revelation was not clear. As a result of prayer, *"the understanding of the message came to him in a vision"* (Daniel 10:1). Daniel had been given a revelation, but did not understand its meaning. He began to pray and fast. He prayed and fasted for 21 days. Then the answer came to him. An angel appeared and gave Daniel the understanding he needed. The angel's words are telling. Look at them closely. *"Do not be afraid, Daniel. Since the first day that you set your mind to gain understanding and to humble yourself before your God, your words were heard, and I have come in response to them"* (Daniel 10:12).

What did Daniel's prayer do?

a. It made God want something He didn't want before.

b. It convinced God to come up with an answer He hadn't yet formulated.

c. It accessed the answer God had ready for Daniel and wanted Daniel to have.

Think about it. God wanted Daniel to know the meaning of the vision. God had everything Daniel needed ready and waiting for him. But why did Daniel have what he needed? The angel said, in essence, "I have come in response to your words." As soon as Daniel began to ask—*"the first day you set your mind to gain understanding"*—the answer was being released. *Because* Daniel prayed, God's will was activated on the earth. Daniel had to ask for what God wanted to give. God's desire to give and Daniel's desire to receive intertwined to form prayer.

Week 3, Day 3

PRACTICE A NEW WAY OF PRAYING

Fix your eyes on Jesus.

DAY FOUR

Look at another instance in Scripture in which prayer clearly activated God's will. To see this fully, we will line up the Old Testament and the New Testament. James 5:16–18 makes a bold statement about prayer. It tells us that prayer changes the earth. It tells us that the spiritual power that prayer releases has authority over the earth. The earth is subject to the power of the Spirit.

The prayer of a righteous man is powerful and effective. —James 5:16

The word translated "powerful and effective" is a Greek word that means "to exercise force; to create change." Prayer has power, and prayer produces an effect. Then, to make his point very clear, James points to an example. He points to Elijah: *"Elijah was a man just like us. He prayed earnestly that it would not rain, and it did not rain on the land for three and a half years. Again he prayed, and the heavens gave rain, and the earth produced its crops"* (James 5:17–18).

James expects his readers to know the story of Elijah. He expects his readers to see that this is a synopsis of the story, not two sentences that stand alone. If you were to read these two sentences without putting them in their bigger setting, it might sound as if Elijah one day decided that a drought would be a good idea and began to ask God for it. This is not the case.

To get the full truth that James is teaching, we will have to put the Old and New Testaments together. We read the story to which James refers in 1 Kings 17. Now, remember that James says that Elijah prayed that it would not rain, and it did not rain. But whose idea is the drought?

Now Elijah the Tishbite, from Tishbe in Gilead, said to Ahab, "As the Lord, *the God of Israel, lives, whom I serve, there will be neither dew nor rain in the next few years except at my word."* —1 Kings 17:1

Elijah makes it clear that he's speaking for God. He prefaces his declaration with a phrase that indicates that Elijah is coming from the presence of his King to deliver his King's message. *"As the Lord God lives, whom I serve..."* His statement is bold and audacious. No dew, no rain, except at Elijah's word. Why can Elijah make such a statement?

Look in 1 Kings 17:24. A widow, whose son Elijah has raised from the dead, makes an observation that explains why Elijah can say, "except at my word." *"Then the woman said to Elijah, 'Now I know that you are a man of God and that the word of the* Lord *from your mouth is the truth.'"*

Elijah's words are God's words. God has declared the drought. What has Elijah done? He has prayed the drought. (1) God says it. (2) Elijah prays it.

(3) God performs it. Elijah's prayers released the will of God on earth.

Then, James says, Elijah's prayers brought rain back to the earth. Whose idea was it for the drought to end? *"After a long time, in the third year, the word of the LORD came to Elijah: 'Go and present yourself to Ahab, and I will send rain on the land'"* (1 Kings 18:1). Once again, God says it, Elijah prays it, God performs it.

Follow the story further. Elijah hears from God. Elijah knows that God is ready to end the drought. He is so certain of this that he declares it publicly. There's no question in Elijah's mind: God wants to end the drought. What does he do? *"And Elijah said to Ahab, 'Go, eat and drink, for there is the sound of a heavy rain.' So Ahab went off to eat and drink, but Elijah climbed to the top of Carmel, bent down to the ground and put his face between his knees"* (1 Kings 18:41–42).

Elijah went off to pray until the word of the Lord was established in the material realm. Elijah knew that prayer was the conduit to bring the will of God from heaven to earth. Elijah knew that his prayers would enforce the will of God, causing the will of God to be done on earth as it was done in heaven. What God had bound in heaven, Elijah's prayer bound on the earth. What God had loosed in heaven, Elijah's prayer loosed on the earth. *"The prayer of a righteous man is powerful and effective"* (James 5:16).

From your study to this point, answer these questions:

What does prayer do?

Can you think of any purpose prayer might have other than to release the power, will, and purposes of God?

Why do you think that God has chosen to work hand-in-hand with His people through prayer?

❖

Week 3, Day 4

PRACTICE A NEW WAY OF PRAYING

Fix your eyes on Jesus.

_____

_____

_____

DAY FIVE

In response to our prayers, spiritual forces are set in motion that bring God's will to earth. Prayer has its first effect in the spiritual realm. When the work is finished in the spiritual realm, the answer is revealed in the material realm.

Prayer is spiritual *work*. What do I mean by that? In the material realm, the definition of "work" is "to use energy to create change." Everything I do that uses energy to create change falls under the category of "work." In the spiritual realm, prayer is how energy is released to create change. Remember James 5:16? *"The prayer of a righteous man is powerful and effective."* Prayer changes the spiritual realm and the spiritual realm changes the material realm. Because prayer has its first effect in the spiritual realm, a reality that cannot be observed with the physical senses, there is a period of time when, from the earth, it appears that prayer isn't changing things. This is because it is doing *spiritual work.* Wait until the time is fulfilled, when everything is ripe. That's when the kingdom of heaven will be revealed to your senses.

Many people mistake prayer for a passive activity. Some think that prayer is what you do when there's nothing left to do *but* pray. My friend, get this deep in your spirit: ***prayer is the work***. Prayer is the most aggressive, offensive, pro-active, invasive work you can ever engage in. We're not talking here about just "saying prayers." This is *living prayer.* Let's examine a well-known, much-quoted passage of Scripture and see what it has to say about prayer as an offensive strategy.

Prayer is spiritual **work.**

Finally, be strong in the Lord and in his mighty power. Put on the full armor of God so that you can take your stand against the devil's schemes. For our struggle is not against flesh and blood, but against the rulers, against the authorities, against the powers of this dark world and against the spiritual forces of evil in the heavenly realms. Therefore put on the full armor of God, so that when the day of evil comes, you may be able to stand your ground, and after you have done everything, to stand. Stand firm then, with the belt of truth buckled around your waist, with the breastplate of righteousness in place, and with your feet fitted with the readiness that comes from the gospel of peace. In addition to all this, take up the shield of faith, with which you can extinguish all the flaming arrows of the evil one. Take the helmet of salvation and the sword of the Spirit, which is the word of God. And pray in the Spirit on all occasions with all kinds of prayers and requests. With this in mind, be alert and always keep on praying for all the saints. —Ephesians 6:10–18

Answer these questions, basing your answers on this passage:

1. What is the thesis statement—the statement that everything else builds from? (The first sentence.)

2. Take this sentence apart; examine each phrase. What is it saying to you?

Be strong

in the Lord

and in His mighty power

3. Paul is about to tell us how to access the power of God for our lives—each situation—and how to sidestep the devil's schemes. Did you know that the devil has a scheme? The word translated "scheme" is a word that means "a well-thought-out plan." The enemy is working according to an agenda. This agenda, this scheme, is being carried out by powers, principalities, and authorities in the spiritual realm. What does Paul say to do? "Therefore, _____ the _____ of God."

4. The word *therefore* links two thoughts together in a cause and effect relationship. Explain the use of *therefore* in this verse. What is the cause? What is the effect?

5. From there, Paul describes the armor. He tells you how to put on the battle gear. Once you have all the armor on, once you are dressed for battle, after he has named the last piece of gear, then what does he say to do?

How do you fight the fight? How do you wield the sword? How do you plunge into enemy-occupied territory? You *pray*! "*And pray in the Spirit on all occasions with all kinds of prayers and requests. With this in mind, be alert and always keep on praying for all the saints*" (Ephesians 6:18).

Prayer Works in the Spiritual Realm
Spirit is the cause of the material realm (Hebrews 11:3) and is the genesis

of activity on the earth. Earth is the reflection or the shadow of activity occurring in the spiritual realm.

For example, Paul teaches us in Ephesians 6:12 that our enemies are not flesh and blood. Rather, they are powers and principalities in the heavenly realms. It would appear that flesh and blood, people, are standing in the way of God's purposes. But Scripture tells us that what we see on the earth is the result of what is happening in the heavenly realms. We also learn that the remedy for what is happening on earth will be accomplished in the spiritual realm. Victories in the spiritual realm result in changes in the physical realm. Earth is subject to the powers of spirit.

God's Word, a Spirit-force, does God's Spirit-work. When God's Spirit-work is finished, it is reflected on the earth. God's Word created the earth and God's Word sustains the earth (Hebrews 1:3). The created is subject to and dependent upon the Creator. The created is physical, but the Creator is Spirit. The material realm is subject to the spiritual realm.

True prayer is God's words in my mouth. God's words do His work and He is sending His words out with an assignment. He is watching over His words to see that the assignment is carried out (Isaiah 55:10–11; Jeremiah 1:9, 12). When God sends His words out through your mouth, the spiritual realm is immediately fully engaged. Spiritual forces are dispatched. All of heaven is poised to respond to the prayers of God's people.

Through prayer, the enemy's schemes are thwarted. Through prayer, the powers, principalities, and authorities of Satan's realm are stopped cold. Through prayer, all of the power and provision of God flows into the lives of His people.

Prayer brings the power of God to earth to do the will of God. Am I saying that God's power is absent from the earth unless I pray? Let's examine this thought more closely. You may be asking, "Is God's power ever absent from the earth?" The answer is "No." His power is never absent. He fills heaven and earth. The earth and its fullness belong to Him. The heavens declare His glory, and creation pours forth knowledge of Him. God's power covers the earth.

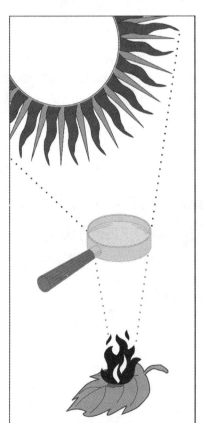

The sun's rays are focused and directed, their power magnified, through a convex lens such as a magnifying glass.

God's specific and intervening power is released into circumstances and lives by prayer. Think of it like this. The sun's rays cover the earth. However, when one holds a magnifying glass over a flammable object, such as a dry leaf, the sun's rays are refracted (bent toward one another) through the glass. The result is that the rays of the sun are concentrated and directed, their power magnified. The refracted rays create focused and intense heat. The leaf, exposed to the focused power of the sun, bursts into flames.

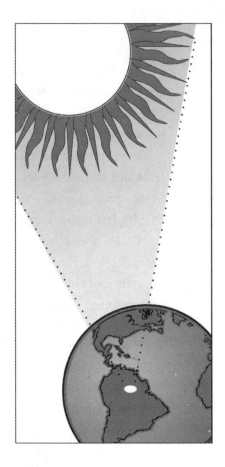

God's power covers the earth. Prayer focuses and magnifies His power on a particular situation or a specific life. That life or situation, consistently exposed to His intense power, is changed by it.

When the sun's rays are captured and refracted through the magnifying glass, has the glass increased or in any way changed the sun's power? No, it has only focused it. The power belongs only to the sun. So it is that prayer focuses the power of God.

Week 3, Day 5

PRACTICE A NEW WAY OF PRAYING

Fix your eyes on Jesus.

_____

_____

_____

_____

_____

_____

Week Three Anniversary Thought

A praying life is fueled by faith. A praying life is faith in action. Prayer accesses faith, and faith is the engine that powers prayer. A life of faith and a praying life are two ways to say the same thing. Paul makes a statement in Romans 4:16: *"The promise comes by faith."*

By using the word *comes*, he is stating that the promise of God will move from one place to another. Break down this thought:

"The promise comes . . .

Comes from where to where? From heaven to earth.

"The promise comes . . ."

How? What is the avenue that brings the promise from heaven to earth?

"The promise comes by faith."

Faith brings the promise out of heaven and makes it reality on earth.

When God puts a promise in you, faith is the process by which that promise is realized in the circumstances of earth. The promise comes by faith. The prayer of faith moves the power and provision of God through the gap and into the circumstances of earth.

The Author of Prayer

PRACTICE A NEW WAY OF PRAYING

This week, each day write out in detail your will for a situation facing you. Write out definite instructions for God about how you think He should handle it. Then write across it in red ink: *Surrendered to the Father. Do Your will in Your way at Your time.* Then pray this way: *Father, here is my will. You know that I have a will and expectations in every matter, but I choose to lay my will down and not settle for anything less than Your wonderful will. I trust Your love for me and Your wisdom in this situation. Not my will, but Yours, be done.*

DAY ONE

In the first place, it is not our prayers that move the Lord Jesus, but the Lord Jesus who moves us to pray. —O. Hallesby, *Prayer*

God initiates prayer. We've turned prayer upside down. Prayer, in the first place, is not me coming to God, but God coming to me. The Scripture tells us that God is awakening desires, initiating spiritual hunger, creating in His children the inclination to seek Him. The Bible tells us that the need we feel that causes us to turn to God—the inner compulsion to pray—is really a response to God's now-speaking voice. From our point of view, it feels like initiative, but it's really response.

Note: Many people ask me about Isaiah 62:6–7, which in the New American Standard says, *"You who remind the Lord, take no rest for yourselves; and give Him no rest until He establishes and makes Jerusalem a praise in the earth."* The word translated "remind" here means "to be in mind of; to remember" (the prefix *re* means to repeat and *mind* means to think or to be mindful; remind—to think again). He is saying, "you who keep the Lord in mind…" Then, look at the preceding verses and you will see that they have been placed in their positions as watchmen on the wall by God. He has initiated their crying out day and night.

He seeks to rouse the spirit of intercession that He may be able to bestow His blessing on mankind. God regards intercession as the highest readiness to receive and to yield themselves wholly to the working of His almighty power. —Andrew Murray, *Prayer*

When you feel the need to pray, do you recognize it as God Himself seeking to rouse the spirit of intercession? Right now, what do you feel compelled to pray about? Write down a topic(s) of concern to you.

Now, go back through each of those topics and let the Spirit of God speak to you about God's longing to bless. Listen to Him tell you that you desire to pray **because He desires to give**. Let the assurance build in your heart that it is the Father Himself inviting you to receive His best in each situation that has caused you to desire to pray. Write out your thoughts.

The only reason that you have an inclination to pray, the only reason that you have any thought that the answer to your longings and your needs might lie with God—**the only reason**—is because God is drawing you. When you pray, you are doing one thing: opening your life to receive His power and provision. Watchman Nee gives a wonderful illustration of this truth in his book, *Let Us Pray*. He suggests that God's will is like a locomotive and our prayers are like a railroad track. A locomotive has all the power necessary to travel from one location to another, but it only travels to places where tracks have been laid.

God has the power to go anywhere He wants to go, but His power only goes where prayer-tracks have been laid. Our prayers fulfill the conditions for the release of His will. Our prayers, in one sense, prepare the way for the Lord, making straight paths for Him (Isaiah 40:3). His power is released by our prayers.

Why do you think that God has designed the workings of the spiritual realm so that prayer is necessary?

Imagine for a moment what life might be like if God automatically did His will without the prayers of His people. How would you recognize His work?

Do you see any way that God's design for prayer reflects His love for His children?

❖

Week 4, Day 1

<u>PRACTICE A NEW WAY OF PRAYING</u>

Write out your will and surrender it to the Father.

_____

_____

_____

_____

_____

DAY TWO

True prayer is when God's heart is expressed through your words. True prayer is when God's words are in your mouth. How do God's words get in your mouth? First, God's desires must be in your heart. "*Out of the overflow of the heart the mouth speaks*" (Matthew 12:34). "*A wise man's heart guides his mouth*" (Proverbs 16:23). Powerful praying is not a matter of knowing the right words to say, rather it is having a heart that is at God's disposal—open to hear His every sigh and whisper and to echo it in prayer. As God molds your heart so that it matches His, your heart overflows in prayer. What God has spoken in your innermost being guides your lips in prayer.

He is your Prayer Teacher. He is transforming your life, shaping your heart. The end result of this intense training is what the Scripture calls "an instructed tongue." "*The Sovereign Lord has given me an instructed tongue*" (Isaiah 50:4).

Paul Billheimer writes, "The content of all true prayer originates in the heart of God." When we are truly praying, we are speaking out the heart of God. Prayer in its highest form occurs when the words I articulate, with my mouth or in my mind, are merely the containers for God's thoughts and desires. When, like Elijah, the Word of the Lord from my mouth is truth, then I am truly praying.

In your prayer experience, how much time have you devoted to making yourself open for God to express Himself to you?

What do you think would be necessary for letting God shape your prayers?

In your own words, what does this sentence mean? "God authors prayer."

Week 4, Day 2

PRACTICE A NEW WAY OF PRAYING
Write out your will and surrender it to the Father.

DAY THREE

In living a praying life, God's will is so exactly reproduced in us that it becomes our will. We find that when we pray the deepest desires of our hearts, we are stating His desires.

The key to being able to receive all that God longs to give is to have a heart that is fully His. When His desires are in our hearts, His words rise from us as prayer. Our job is to allow the Spirit of God the access He needs to each of our hearts so He can cleanse them of debris. The clutter in our hearts throws off its acoustics. *Acoustics* are defined as "the qualities that determine the ability of an enclosure to reflect sound waves in such a way as to produce distinct hearing." How are your heart's acoustics? Does God need to do some renovation? Does He need to tear down some walls? Clear out some rubbish? Haul away some wreckage? Clean out some corners?

Read John 15:7. What is the one central key that opens your life to all that God longs to give you?

Listen to God. Ask Him if your life is as open to Him as possible. What is the Spirit of God surfacing in your thoughts? How can your life become more open to what God wants to give? Write down what you hear Him say.

❖

Week 4, Day 3

PRACTICE A NEW WAY OF PRAYING

Write out your will and surrender it to the Father.

_____

_____

_____

_____

DAY FOUR

The Scripture teaches that God has created you so that you can contain His Spirit. When His Spirit makes His home in you, He then speaks in you and makes known to you all truth. Let me lay out for you the logic for believing that Almighty God can and will speak to you.

1. God designed prayer. God put prayer into effect to function as the conduit that brings His will out of the spiritual realm and causes it to take effect on the earth.

2. God wants to do His will.

3. Prayer works when it is the expression of His will. (Read 1 John 5:14–15.)

4. God did not set us up for failure. He designed prayer to work effectively.

5. Therefore, _God can make His will and His desires known to us._

The key to everything is that the life of Jesus is flowing through you by means of His Spirit. It is Jesus' prayers that are the content of your prayers. The Spirit is reproducing the intercession of Jesus in you. **Jesus is the praying life**, and His life is in you.

We do this because we are partakers of His life—"Christ is our life," "No longer I, but Christ liveth in me." The life in Him and in us is one and the same. His life in heaven is an ever-praying life. When it descends and takes possession of us, it does not lose its character; in us too it is the ever-praying life—a life that without ceasing asks and receives from God.... As we know that Jesus communicates His whole life in us, He also, out of that prayerfulness which is His alone, breathes into us our praying.
— **Andrew Murray,** *The Secret of Believing Prayer*

If Jesus dwells at the source of my life—if the flow of His life has replaced all of my life—then He can safely commit the praying to my will. If absolute obedience to Him is the inspiration and force of every movement of my life, then He will pledge Himself, by a duty as deep as His own nature, that whatever is asked will be granted.
— **E. M. Bounds,** *The Necessity of Prayer*

Read 1 Corinthians 2:12. For what clearly expressed purpose have we received "the Spirit who is from God"?

Read 1 Corinthians 2:16. Where is "the mind of Christ"?

Read John 16:13–15. What does Jesus promise that the Holy Spirit will do?

When Jesus says that the Spirit will "*take from what is mine and make it known to you*," do you think that includes Jesus' intercession? Will the Holy Spirit make known Jesus' prayers to you so that you can join Him?

Week 4, Day 4

PRACTICE A NEW WAY OF PRAYING

Write out your will and surrender it to the Father.

_____

_____

_____

_____

_____

DAY FIVE

God's heart is the beginning point of prayer. Any request that does not begin with God is not true prayer. The content of our prayers is God's decision. Ezekiel 36:37 illustrates this truth. Here, through the prophet Ezekiel, God is foretelling the end of the days of Judah's judgment. In preceding verses He has described His plan to restore Israel. The plan was not yet so on the earth, but it was firmly fixed in the heart of God. He describes it in detail. Then in verse 37 (NASB) He says: "This also will I let the house of Israel ask Me to do for them." Do you see? Part of God's whole plan is that Israel will ask for what God longs to give. God Himself will author their prayers.

Prayer releases onto the earth what God has prepared in heaven. The answer is prepared before the request is made. In fact, the answer is prepared before the need occurs. _"Before they call I will answer; while they are still speaking I will hear"_ (Isaiah 65:24).

God wants to author our prayers in such a way that He will be glorified. Psalm 50:15 says, _"Call to me in the day of trouble; I will deliver you, and you will honor me."_ When we call to Him, releasing His power and His will, He will be able to bring honor to Himself. He wants our lives to become billboards upon which He can advertise Himself. He wants our lives to be stages upon which He can perform. He wants our lives to be trophy cases in which He can display His mighty deeds. He wants us to be living proof of Him. Through prayer we give Him permission to act in our lives in a way that will show His power and authority.

Read 1 Corinthians 2:9 and Ephesians 3:20. How does God describe what He wants to do in our lives?

Does God want to do the best thing you can imagine?

God wants to do *more* than you can imagine. Do you really want to limit God to what you can think up? If we could get God to do what we think He should do when we think He should do it, we would miss the eternal plan that exceeds our imaginations.

Consider the story of Lazarus in John 11. Lazarus was very ill, on his deathbed, and Mary and Martha sent an urgent message to Jesus: *"The one you love is sick."* The implication in their message, and their expectation, was that Jesus should quickly make His way to Bethany and heal Lazarus before he died. Jesus did not act in accordance with their expectations of Him. He did not hurry to Bethany to heal Lazarus before he died.

Four days elapsed between the time that Lazarus died and the time that Jesus arrived. You can imagine what a devastating four days it was. Imagine the disillusionment and disappointment Mary and Martha felt when Jesus failed to meet their expectations. Everything they believed about Jesus at that moment was threatened. Have you ever been in that state? Have you ever been in a situation that, after looking at all the empirical evidence and all the facts, the only conclusion you could reach was that God had let you down? That's where Mary and Martha were. They were experiencing a crisis of faith.

What did Jesus plan to do? He planned to do **more** *than they could think or imagine.*

Let's look at Mary's and Martha's faith. Both expressed their firm belief that if Jesus had been there, Lazarus would not have died (vv. 21, 32). They thought that in asking Jesus to heal Lazarus, they had asked all that it was possible to ask. They thought that healing Lazarus was pushing the limits of His power. Once Lazarus was dead, they reasoned, Jesus was too late. They had asked all that they could think or imagine.

What did Jesus plan to do? He planned to do *more* than they could think or imagine. He was not interested in meeting their expectations because He intended to exceed their expectations. He did not confirm their faith, because He wanted to stretch their faith. He was not content to leave Mary and Martha with what they knew of Him so far. By raising Lazarus from the dead, He enlarged their understanding of Him and their view of His power. When God has access to our needs, He will always show us something new about Himself. We will learn to align ourselves with eternal realities and not have our faith sabotaged by time-bound, earth-bound vision. We will begin to live beyond our limits.

Are you trying to hold God to the best thing you can think of? Right now, would you tell God that you are aligning yourself with the best thing He can think of? That you are open to His best, even if it conflicts with your own earth-bound expectations? Write out your thoughts.

Week 4, Day 5

PRACTICE A NEW WAY OF PRAYING

Write out your will and surrender it to the Father.

_____

_____

_____

_____

_____

_____

_____

_____

Week Four Anniversary Thought

Consider a sponge. It has a molecular makeup that predisposes it to be absorbent. When a sponge comes into contact with a liquid, the sponge soaks up all of the liquid it can hold. That's just the nature of a sponge. A sponge, because of its design, can't keep from absorbing liquid. A sponge that has come into contact with liquid becomes saturated with that liquid. Everything about the liquid—all its chemical components and its color and smell and taste—is now soaked into the sponge. The sponge is the container of the liquid.

When we were born again and became new creations, we were given a spiritual makeup that, when we come into contact with the living God, will absorb as much of Him as we can hold. His thoughts will transform our thoughts. His heart will reform our hearts. His desires will reshape our desires. We can partake of the divine nature. We have the mind of Christ. The Spirit reveals the deep things of God.

As God authors our prayers, He doesn't just dictate to us. He changes us. As we purposefully keep our lives soaked in His presence, He will give Himself to us.

Section Two

The Process of Prayer

The Process of Prayer

PRACTICE A NEW WAY OF PRAYING

Each day's prayer journal activity will have a Scripture reference that describes some aspect of God's nature. Look up the reference, consider His ways, and, as you pray, let His nature provide a foothold for your faith.

DAY ONE

As I continued in the school of prayer, I recognized another misconception that was limiting my prayer life. I had assumed that prayer was made up of two parts: my request and God's answer. I thought the measure of my prayer ability was how many times I received what I asked for. I had what I now think of as a "prayer list prayer life."

What do I mean by a prayer list prayer life? This is a mind-set that limits prayer to getting God to perform for you. Understand, there's nothing wrong with a prayer list. In fact, a prayer list is a wonderful tool for observing God's power. It all depends on how you use it. The problem occurs when your prayer list is really a "To Do List" for God. Let me illustrate this subtle error in thinking by telling you a story about my son Brantley. Brantley was about three years old when he and I were driving down a very busy street in Atlanta. It seemed that every time we pulled up to a red light, it changed to green. The lights were with us. Finally, Brantley could not contain his delight any longer. "Mom!" he said with great enthusiasm. "I've been praying for God to change the lights and He's been obeying me!" You and I know too much about theology to use the word "obey," but if we're honest, that's really how we're seeing it. If God did what was on my list, He answered. If He didn't do what was on my list, He didn't answer, or He said no. And this became the measure of prayer's effectiveness.

A "prayer list prayer life" begins to build a distorted understanding of prayer. According to the prayer list, sometimes God says yes and sometimes God says no. Since the praying person would have no way of knowing whether this is a time when God will say yes, or this is a time when God will say no, it becomes very hard to pray boldly and confidently.

As you are learning to live a praying life, prayer takes on a much broader definition than "saying prayers." Much of what prayer is accomplishing cannot be condensed to a list. Many times the direct answers to petitions are the least important aspect of what the prayer accomplished. I believe that as you progress and mature into a praying life, your testimony of prayer's effectiveness will be that the mercies of God unfold at every turn. You walk in answered prayer. O. Hallesby states it like this: "The longer you live a life of this kind, the more answers to prayer you will experience. As white snow flakes fall quietly and thickly on a winter's day, answers to prayer will settle down on you at every step you take, even to your dying day."

Prayer lists are effective if they are in the context of a praying life. Use your prayer list like this: Write down the concern or the need and date it. The date is the day you surrendered it to God for His purposes, His ways, and His timing. Now, don't watch to see *if* God answers; watch to see *how* God answers. You will find that He answers progressively. He puts together pieces, each one building on the other. Record things as you go along and watch with amazement as God pieces things together for an outcome that is more than you could think or imagine.

Take inventory of your thoughts and attitudes about prayer. Have you had a "prayer list prayer life"? Do you have a mental file of all the times God didn't follow your instructions? Is that mental file insidiously undermining your faith in God and your boldness in prayer? Write out your thoughts.

Prayer *cannot* be summed up in a simple two-part equation: my request + God's answer = prayer. Prayer is a process. Webster's dictionary defines the word "process" as "a natural phenomenon marked by gradual changes that lead toward a particular result; a series of actions or operations conducing to an end." It is during the process of prayer that God does His mightiest work. If this were not so, then God would have set prayer up to work like a vending machine: put in a request, get out an answer. God has a loving and productive reason for the process of prayer.

Week 5, Day 1

PRACTICE A NEW WAY OF PRAYING

But the eyes of the LORD are on those who fear him, on those whose hope is in his unfailing love. —Psalm 33:18

_____

_____

_____

_____

_____

DAY TWO

It is during the process of prayer that the praying person is brought to total submission to the Father. During the process of prayer, God weans our hearts from the things we so desire to fasten on Him.

At our first entrance into the school of waiting upon God, the heart is chiefly set upon the blessings which we wait for. God graciously uses our need and desire for help to educate us for something higher than we were thinking of. We were seeking gifts; He, the Giver, longs to give Himself and to satisfy the soul with His goodness.
—Andrew Murray, *Waiting On God*

God works through the prayer process to expand our vision, to deepen our hunger, to stretch our faith, and to lift our desires higher. We start the process desiring something from Him; we end it desiring only Him. Through the prayer process, our heart's cry becomes, *"Whom have I in heaven but you? And earth has nothing I desire besides you. My flesh and my heart may fail, but God is the strength of my heart and my portion forever"* (Psalm 73:25–26).

When the Prayer Teacher has been able to reveal to you that He is all, that there is nothing to crave but more of Him, then you realize that He is willing to answer every prayer with a "yes"—because the heart of every true prayer is: "More of You. More of You." Your need or your desire is simply the entry point for Him to give you more of Himself. In meeting your need and fulfilling your desire, He is drawing you to deeper dependence on Him, therefore to deeper intimacy with Him.

What is your concern or need or desire right now? Where do you long to see God demonstrate His power?

Would you be willing to make this your prayer? *Father, I confess that I have set my heart on an outcome rather than on You. Right now, in the power of Your indwelling life, I transfer my hope and expectation to You. The heart of my prayer is, "More of You." I ask You to work in this matter in whatever way will bring me more of You.*

Week 5, Day 2

PRACTICE A NEW WAY OF PRAYING

The Lord is righteous in all his ways and loving toward all he has made. The Lord is near to all who call on him, to all who call on him in truth.
—Psalm 145:17–18

_____

_____

_____

_____

_____

DAY THREE

Psalm 37:4 says, "*Delight yourself in the Lord and he will give you the desires of your heart.*" During the process of prayer, this truth takes on its richest, deepest meaning.

First, you find that when you delight yourself in the Lord, He *becomes* the desire of your heart. The word translated "delight" comes from a Hebrew root word that means "soft, moldable, or pliable." When you delight yourself in the Lord, you become pliable and moldable in His hands. He is able to fashion a heart like His. He is able to create desires that match His will. In fact, Paul writes, "*It is God who works in you to will…his good purpose*" (Philippians 2:13).

Second, you realize that you cannot know the desire of your heart unless you know the heart of your desire. Usually, what we call "the desire of my heart" is really a secondary desire orbiting around the true desire. Usually, what we think we desire is really the way we have imagined the true desire will be met. Let me first give you a simple illustration of what I mean.

My son Kennedy played on the freshman football team. They often had games on Wednesday nights. Skipping the games was not an option since he had made a commitment to the team. At our church, Wednesday night is the night geared toward youth who are lost. One Wednesday night a quarter, we have a youth baptism. On a particular Wednesday night scheduled for youth baptism, two boys whom Kennedy had led to Christ were to be baptized, but Kennedy had a football game. So, Kennedy and I prayed that God would rain out the game. Now, why did we pray that? It wasn't that we really desired rain; it was that we wanted Kennedy to get to see his friends baptized. But we couldn't think of anything else that would cancel a freshman football game.

I'll make my long story short. It didn't rain. Did God say no to our prayer? The game started and it became dark. The field lights malfunctioned and the game had to be called. Kennedy made it to church in plenty of time to see and to celebrate his friends' baptisms. Do you see? Our prayer was that it would rain, but our desire was that Kennedy would attend the baptisms. Some day I will learn once and for all that God does not need my suggestions, just my prayers. But, while I'm learning, He is always saying yes to my heart's desire.

On a much deeper level than the story I just told, the same dynamic is happening. We think we are asking for the desire of our hearts, but we are really asking for the desire of the moment. Often, in order to give you the desire of your heart, God will withhold the desire of the moment. He only says no as a prelude to a higher yes. Give Him time—give Him access—so that He can peel back the desire of the moment and show you the desire of your heart. To the desire of your heart, there will always be a resounding yes from heaven.

I began to learn this one time when I had finished leading a conference in New Mexico, during which my body encountered unfamiliar allergens against which it rebelled. My voice got raspier and raspier as the conference went on. By the time I had finished, I had no voice at all. I had to leave the next morning and fly to Kentucky, where I would begin to lead another conference. On the flight, I prayed, "Oh, God, give me back my voice." The Lord began to ask me, "Why do you want your voice?" I answered, "So I can lead this conference."

"Why do you want to lead the conference?"

"So that people can learn how to live in Your power."

"Why do you want people to live in My power?"

Give Him time—give Him access—so that He can peel back the desire of the moment and show you the desire of your heart.

"So You can glorify Yourself."

"Then, Jennifer," He seemed to say, "ask Me for that."

And my prayer became, "Father, glorify Yourself."

The tension left me. My soul rested. I did not know how God would answer my prayer, but I knew that He would answer my prayer. He helped me discover the desire of my heart and relinquish the desire of the moment.

Read 2 Corinthians 12:7–10 and answer the following questions.

1. What was Paul's request? (v. 8)

2. Did God say no to that specific request?

3. What was the heart of Paul's desire? In other words, why did he want the thorn in his flesh removed?

4. What was Paul's true heart's desire? (Philippians 3:7–11 will give you a good idea.)

5. Did God say yes to the desire of Paul's heart?

Paul's prayer was stated in words that expressed the desire of the moment—to be rid of the thorn in his flesh that seemed to hinder his work. But the wonderful Father heard the cry of Paul's heart: to know Him fully—both in the power of His resurrection and in the fellowship of His suffering—and to be conformed into His image. In order to give Paul the desire of his heart, God had to withhold the desire of the moment. What looks like a no is really a yes in disguise. If you are crying out for bread, He will not give you a stone (Matthew 7:9). He will not give you something that just resembles your true desire. He will not give you something just to pacify you. He will give you your true heart's desire in order to satisfy you.

God never says no to the desire of your heart. As you surrender yourself to the process of prayer, let Him have so much access to you that He is able to clear away all the secondary desires. Let Him crystallize for you and bring to the forefront the one overriding desire—to have more of Him. *"As for me, the nearness of God is my good"* (Psalm 73:28 NASB).

Week 5, Day 3

PRACTICE A NEW WAY OF PRAYING

As a father has compassion on his children, so the LORD has compassion on those who fear him; for he knows how we are formed, he remembers that we are dust. —Psalm 103:13–14

_____

_____

_____

_____

_____

DAY FOUR

E. Stanley Jones uses a phrase that I think perfectly describes what happens during the process of prayer. He says that God "shifts the whole center of gravity of the prayer."

Just as the moon cannot be reflected well on a restless sea, so God cannot get to an unquiet mind. "Be still and know"; be not still and you do not know—God cannot get to you. In the stillness the prayer itself may be corrected. For God does not only answer prayer; He also corrects prayer and makes it more answerable. One night I bowed my head in silent prayer before a sermon and whispered to God, "O God, help me." Very quickly came back the reply: "I will do something better; I will use you."

That amendment was decidedly better. I was asking God to help me—I was the center; I was calling to God for my own purposes. But "I will use you" meant I was not the center; something beyond me was the

center and I was only the instrument of that purpose beyond myself. God's answer shifted the whole center of gravity of the prayer.

—E. Stanley Jones, *Abundant Living*

As we look at the process of prayer over the next few weeks, you will clearly see that the process is beneficial. You will welcome the process instead of resisting it. You will learn how to let it develop perseverance in you and how to let the process *"finish its work so that you may be mature and complete, not lacking anything"* (James 1:4).

What God is accomplishing during the process of prayer will set you free from anxiety, from insecurity, from fear, from discouragement, from everything that holds any mastery over you. He is setting you free from limited thinking. He Himself is teaching you the deep truth that sets you free. *"You will know the truth, and the truth will set you free....If the Son sets you free, you will be free indeed"* (John 8:32, 36).

What emotions do you think have mastery over you? What emotions seem able to take you captive at will?

Surrender each of these emotions to the Son and ask Him to use the process of prayer to set you truly free. Ask Him to make the truth real for you.

Week 5, Day 4

PRACTICE A NEW WAY OF PRAYING

He will not let your foot slip—he who watches over you will not slumber; indeed, he who watches over Israel will neither slumber nor sleep.

—Psalm 121:3–4

DAY FIVE

The process of prayer resembles the process of pregnancy and birth. Paul stated it like this: *"My dear children, for whom I am again in the pains of childbirth until Christ is formed in you"* (Galatians 4:19).

Notice here two sides of the process of prayer. During the process, God is at work in us shaping us into the image of Christ. The word translated "form" here is a Greek word that means "to form, fashion, originally used of artists who shaped their material into an image." The Scripture is using an imagery that is consistent throughout—the image of the Master Potter sculpting and shaping clay into the form He desires. The process of prayer results in change in us. During the process of prayer, He is fashioning a heart like His.

Second, Paul describes his experience in praying God's will for the Galatians as similar to childbirth. He is in labor, he says, until the will of God is delivered from the spiritual realm to the material realm. Remember when we examined Elijah's prayer in 1 Kings 18:42: *"Elijah climbed to the top of Carmel, bent down to the ground and put his face between his knees."* Do you know what Elijah was doing? He was taking the birthing position. The passage goes on to describe Elijah's travail. He continued in prayer until his servant could report to him that a cloud small as a man's hand had appeared in earth's sky. Then Elijah knew that God's will had been brought through the gap and released on the earth.

Why do you think God, in His Word, pictures prayer as a birthing process? What is He teaching us?

Week 5, Day 5

PRACTICE A NEW WAY OF PRAYING

As for God, his way is perfect; the word of the LORD is flawless. He is a shield for all who take refuge in him. —Psalm 18:30

_____

_____

_____

Week Five Anniversary Thought

The Potter is shaping your heart so that it is the container for His desires. He is creating a masterpiece of His own design. He is forming a vessel into which He will pour out His heart.

> *If you had responded to my rebuke,*
> *I would have poured out my heart to you*
> *and made my thoughts known to you.*
> —Proverbs 1:23

Do you see God's desire? He wants to make His thoughts known to you. It delights Him when we place ourselves in His hands, letting Him mold us, so that He can shape us as it seems best to Him (see Jeremiah 18:4).

The Potter needs clay that is soft and yielded. It is the Potter's hands you feel shaping you—squeezing, pushing, pinching. He knows exactly what He is doing. You can entrust yourself to Him without fear or reservation. Your work is just to surrender. Be transformed.

Waiting on God

PRACTICE A NEW WAY OF PRAYING

This week as you pray, thank God for your waiting periods. Surrender yourself to His timing and recognize it as perfect. Let Him speak to you from His Word. Each day, write out what you hear Him saying to you about your specific situation. Let Him call you by name and tell you His thoughts. Journal your thoughts and insights.

DAY ONE

The most difficult part of the process of prayer can be waiting on God. When we fail to recognize the waiting time as an indispensable ingredient in the process, it becomes a time of discouragement and frustration. It is during the waiting times that many people drop out of the school of prayer. Not receiving their answers as they expected, many conclude that prayer doesn't work, at least not for them.

While the waiting time is the most difficult part of the process, it is also the most important. Waiting gives God the opportunity to redefine our desires and align our purpose and vision with His. What appears from the earth-perspective to be a delay on God's part is really the time when God is working in the spiritual realm, beyond our senses. "*Faith is being...certain of what we do not see*" (Hebrews 11:1). During the waiting time, we are operating by faith. We'll explore faith in more depth during Week Ten.

Prayer has an immediate impact. The instant a thought is turned toward God, no matter how unformed or inarticulate the thought, it creates a stir in the heavenly realms. Unless we understand what is happening in the spiritual realm, we may think that prayer is having no effect. Prayer impacts the spiritual realm and the spiritual realm impacts the earth.

Let me explain what I mean. Paul writes, "*So we fix our eyes not on what is seen, but on what is unseen....We live by faith, not by sight*" (2 Corinthians 4:18; 5:7). Paul contrasts "faith" and "sight." They are opposites, he says. He is saying that physical sight, being able to observe something with our earth-eyes, is not the ground and basis of what we know to be true. We can know things that we cannot see.

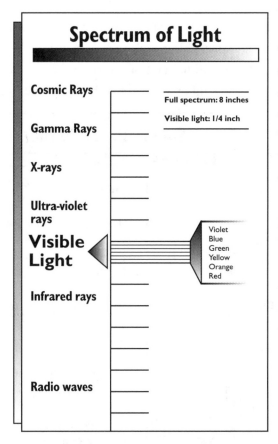

Spectrum of Light

Cosmic Rays

Gamma Rays

X-rays

Ultra-violet rays

Visible Light

Infrared rays

Radio waves

Full spectrum: 8 inches

Visible light: 1/4 inch

Violet
Blue
Green
Yellow
Orange
Red

He also contrasts physical vision and spiritual vision. Obviously we cannot *"fix our eyes… on what is unseen"* unless he means our spiritual eyes. So we conclude that our spiritual eyes can see spiritual reality just like our earth-eyes can see material reality.

Faith is spiritual sight, but not physical sight. Faith produces an understanding that surpasses what we can understand by observing material facts. *"By faith we understand that the universe was formed at God's command, so that what is seen was not made out of what was visible"* (Hebrews 11:3). Without faith—spiritual sight—we cannot understand the full truth. We will see only a fragment of reality.

For example, suppose that I decided that I want to understand the truth about light. I would observe light carefully over a period of time and would eventually reach a conclusion based on my observations. I would conclude that light is what I can see. If I can see it, it's light. If I can't see it, it's not light.

This conclusion would be so limited that it would be untrue. It would fall so far short of the truth about light that it would be false. You see, light includes in it elements and power that I cannot observe. Light rays include gamma rays, but I can't observe them with my eyes. Light includes x-rays, ultraviolet rays, infrared rays, radio waves—but I can't see them. If the spectrum of light were represented in a diagram eight inches long, only one quarter of one inch would represent visible light. If I decided to define light based on what I could see, I would never know the power of light.

The spectrum of our reality includes elements and power I cannot see with my earth-eyes. Reality is made up of both what I can see and what I can't see. My reality includes the power of God, the plans and purposes of God, the present-tense voice of God, and the promises of God. The spectrum of my reality includes the sovereignty of God, the lordship and authority of Jesus, the work of the Spirit, angels, Satan, and the hierarchy of Satan's realm. The portion of reality that I can see—earth and the circumstances of earth—are only a miniscule portion of the whole continuum of reality. If I base my definition of reality on what I can observe on the earth, I will never comprehend the full reality. In the life of faith, circumstances never fully define reality.

Prayer impacts the invisible, spiritual end of the spectrum. The spiritual end of the spectrum impacts the material end. We are to focus our attention on what God is doing in the spiritual end of the spectrum of reality, confident that His activity will show up on the earth at the right time in the right way.

What we can observe from earth is only the appearance; it is not the truth. Faith acts in harmony with truth and disregards appearance. The circumstances of earth are like an optical illusion. When you look at an optical illusion, your eyes tell you one thing, but the truth is something else. You can only interpret an optical illusion correctly if you understand the principles of how the background affects the foreground. You have to *know* something that you do not see. Otherwise, you will believe a lie.

This week we will examine what the Scripture tells us God is doing when it looks to us like He's delaying. Do you believe that God has a good and productive purpose for building waiting periods into your life? Recall James 1:2–4: "*Consider it pure joy, my brothers, whenever you face trials of many kinds, because you know that the testing of your faith develops perseverance. Perseverance must finish its work so that you may be mature and complete, not lacking anything.*"

When God brings waiting periods into your life it is for only one reason: so that you can test-drive your faith. If I were planning to buy a car, I could research my purchase and decide what car I wanted—what make and model, what color, what add-on features. I could know everything about the car I want *except* how it handles in my hands. Not until I get behind the wheel and drive it for myself will I know the feel of the car. I have to drive it myself before I can know exactly how to adjust the seat and the mirrors, or how much pressure I have to put on the brake pedal to bring it to smooth stop, or exactly how I have to turn the steering wheel to get exactly the right angle when I turn. I won't make my final purchase until I've handled the car myself—until I've test-driven it. It's the same way with your faith. You

Spectrum of Reality

Sovereignty of God

Lordship and authority of Jesus

Angels, surrounding the throne, crying "Holy, Holy, Holy"

Angels, ministering spirits sent to minister to the heirs of salvation

Angels fighting spiritual battles against forces of Satan's realm

Visible Reality

Earth: Material, physical objects
Circumstances of earthly life

Satan: The spirit of rebellion now at work in the sons of disobedience can study faith. You can memorize verses about faith. You can learn slick, pithy definitions about faith. But until you have the opportunity to test-drive your own faith, you will never know how it handles in your hands. James says that God "tests" our faith. Does that mean He puts it to the test so that He can see how much faith you have? Or does He put it to the test so that you can see how faith operates? The word "test" really means "to prove." God knows everything about you and everything that's in your heart. In fact, He knows it better than you do. He doesn't have to devise a test that will tell Him about your faith. He is proving your faith to you! Peter says the same thing: *"These [i.e., trials] have come so that your faith—of greater worth than gold, which perishes even though refined by fire—may be proved genuine and may result in praise, glory and honor when Jesus Christ is revealed"* (1 Peter 1:7; author's comments added).

When God allows you to test-drive your faith over and over again, you learn how to operate in faith with confidence. You become a mature and seasoned faith-walker. Mature faith has deep roots. It is not easily shaken. The person with mature faith is steady and tenacious. He has what James calls "perseverance," the ability to go the distance.

Rows of beautiful trees were laid low in a storm. Reason? The water was too near the surface; so the trees did not have to put their roots deep down to find water; hence the tragedy. God may deny us a surface answer in order to get us to put our roots deeper into eternal reality, so that in some future storm we shall be unmoved.
—**E. Stanley Jones,** *Abundant Living*

What is it that you are waiting for? What is your proving ground right now?

Do you believe that God has the power to change your circumstances and end your wait right now?

Do you believe that God loves you and wants only your highest good and deepest happiness?

1. **If** God has the power to change your circumstances right now; and

2. **If** God loves you and wants your highest good; and

3. **If** the circumstances are still in place;

4. **Then** what is your conclusion, based on truth?

❖

Week 6, Day 1

PRACTICE A NEW WAY OF PRAYING

Thank God for every day of your wait, grounding your thanksgiving in His Word.

Moses answered them, "Wait until I find out what the LORD *commands concerning you."* —Numbers 9:8

DAY TWO

Today we will continue to look at what is happening in the spiritual realm while from the earth it appears that God is delaying. Let me repeat a thought. Get this firmly in the forefront of your thinking. Filter everything else through this truth: In response to prayer, God is *always* bringing His will into being.

Because God has set up the cosmos so that prayer brings His power into the circumstances of earth, it is clear that He wants to work through His people, not outside them. He wants His people engaged in what He's doing. He wants to make His will known to His people so that they can pray it. However, He does not submit to us His detailed plan for how He is going to do His will. If we don't understand that, sometimes during the waiting period it will look as though God has lost control of events and everything is headed in the wrong direction. Let's dig deeper into the lessons we learn about God's ways from the story of Joseph.

Joseph's Example

God wants you to understand His will. He wants you to have "*the full riches of complete understanding*" (Colossians 2:2). He has given His Spirit so that "*we may understand what God has freely given us*" (1 Corinthians 2:12). Jesus has come and "*has given us understanding, so that we may know him who is true*" (1 John 5:20). He wants to "*fill you with the knowledge of his will through all spiritual wisdom and understanding*" (Colossians 1:9).

Does it sound as if God is keeping His will a secret? On the contrary, He has made every provision for you to know His will. He wants you to know His will. He invites you to know His will. In fact, understanding His will is the cornerstone of power praying. You cannot pray with power if you do not pray according to His will. Since He designed prayer to be the conduit that brings His power to earth, and since He designs all things perfectly, He plans for you to know His will. He plans for prayer to work.

The path His will takes, the way He brings His will into being, remains a mystery. "*Oh, the depth of the riches of the wisdom and knowledge of God! How unsearchable his judgments, and his paths beyond tracing out!*" (Romans 11:33). God will never hand over to us His all-knowingness. Sometimes we mistake His will for His ways and become confused. When I think that I have reached an understanding of God's will and begin to pray according to it, He often begins bringing His will about in a way that looks to me like a mistake. I have now built up enough history with Him that usually I know to wait and watch—not to confuse His *ways* with His *will*. I'm learning not to confuse what He's doing with how He's doing it.

Consider the story of Joseph, which begins in the thirty-seventh chapter of Genesis and continues through the first chapter of Exodus. What was God's will for Joseph? God showed Joseph His plan in a series of dreams. Joseph came to understand that he was destined to be a ruler to whom even his father and brothers would bow. The next we hear of Joseph, he is at the bottom of a well listening to his brothers plot his death and begging for his life (Genesis 42:21). He is sold into slavery, taken as a slave to a foreign land, and thrown into prison after being falsely accused. It does not appear that God is bringing about His will. It appears that God has lost control of Joseph's life because of the choices of evil men. Actually, God is working out His plan for Joseph so that He can work out His plan for Israel so that He can work out His plan for humanity.

For God's perspective on the situation, look at Psalm 105. What is God's will for Israel, the nation? Read verses 8–11. Summed up, it is this: "*To you I will give the land of Canaan as the portion you will inherit*" (v. 11). When Israel first reached Canaan, they were "*but few in number, few indeed, and strangers in it, they wandered from nation to nation, from one kingdom to another*" (vv.12–13). What did God need to do in order to bring His will about? He needed to give Israel a place to grow, prosper, learn skills, and reproduce safely. He needed to put them under the protection of a larger, more advanced civilization for a time. He needed them in Egypt.

How did He do it? *"He sent a man before them—Joseph, sold as a slave"* (Psalm 105:17). It looked as if Joseph's evil brothers had sent him to Egypt. It looked as if God's will was being thwarted by bad decisions. But God said that it was He who sent Joseph to Egypt. Joseph explained it to his brothers like this: *"But God sent me ahead of you to preserve for you a remnant on earth and to save your lives by a great deliverance. So then, it was not you who sent me here, but God"* (Genesis 45:7–8). God used seemingly adverse circumstances to position Joseph for receiving the promise.

How did God get Israel out of Canaan into Egypt? *"He called down famine on the land and destroyed all their supplies of food"* (Psalm 105:16). He brought famine on the land, but first He prepared their deliverance. It was waiting for them in Egypt. What appeared to be a disaster and a tragedy drove them to God's provision.

How was God bringing about His will for Joseph and at the same time bringing His plan for His people into being? God allowed Joseph to be put in a position from which God could display His power in just the way that would give Joseph the most credibility with the pharaoh. *"They bruised his feet with shackles, his neck was put in irons, till what he foretold came to pass, till the word of the LORD proved him true. The king sent and released him, the ruler of peoples set him free. He made him master of his household, ruler over all he possessed, to instruct his princes as he pleased and teach his elders wisdom"* (Psalm 105:18–22). Did God bring about exactly what He had promised Joseph He would do? Yes, to the last detail. Did God do it as Joseph expected Him to? No, far from it.

When God had Joseph in place, when He had brought about His plan for Joseph, His Joseph-plan could merge with His Israel-plan. Israel moved into Egypt under the protection of Joseph, whom God had put in place. In Egypt, the tiny nation of Israel grew to become a large nation. *"Then Israel entered Egypt.... The LORD made his people very fruitful"* (vv. 23–24).

Exodus chapter one tells us that the nation of Israel grew so large and so strong that it frightened the new king. *"'Look' he said to his people, 'the Israelites have become much too numerous for us. Come, we must deal shrewdly with them or they will become even more numerous and, if war breaks out, will join our enemies, fight against us and leave the country.' So they put slave masters over them to oppress them with forced labor"* (Exodus 1:9–11).

What was the next step in God's plan for His people? He wanted to toughen them up—physically, mentally, and spiritually—and get them ready to take the land He had promised from their enemies. So what did He do? *"The Lord made his people very fruitful; he made them too numerous for their foes, **whose hearts he turned to hate his people**, to conspire against his servants"* (Psalm 105:24–25). Do you see? It appeared that the Israelites became victims to the whim of the new pharaoh. The truth is that God was moving Israel forward. He was engineering Israel's next step toward possessing the promise. What looked like a setback was really a step forward. He had grown the nation of Israel in number. Now He wanted to grow them in character. When they were ready, He wanted them to possess the promise. He wanted to drive them out of Egypt, the land to which they had become accustomed, and propel them into the Land of the Promise.

God's plan was that Israel would be the channel for His will into all the nations of the earth. God's will is not short-term, but flows from generation to generation.

How God does His will is up to Him. You cannot control God or tell Him how to accomplish His plan. He will do His will in His way.

Oh, the depth of the riches of the wisdom and knowledge of God! How unsearchable his judgments, and his paths beyond tracing out! Who has known the mind of the Lord? Or who has been his counselor?
—Romans 11:33–34

"Does the clay say to the potter, 'What are you making?'…It is I who made the earth and created mankind upon it." —Isaiah 45:9, 12

Who has understood the mind of the Lord, or instructed him as his counselor? Whom did the Lord consult to enlighten him, and who taught him the right way? —Isaiah 40:13–14

As you do not know the path of the wind, or how the body is formed in a mother's womb, so you cannot understand the work of God, the Maker of all things. —Ecclesiastes 11:5

When you treat prayer as if you have the right to tell God how to do His work, you will be disappointed. God does not take instructions. When you realize that God's ways are not your ways, that His ways are superior to your ways, you will not be thrown off balance when circumstances seem to be leading away from God's will rather than toward it. You can trust that God is steadily moving forward in the direction of His will.

God's will is not short-term, but flows from generation to generation.

Do you have any circumstances in your life in which it appears that God is taking the situation away from the direction of His will? In other words, is there anything that seems to be getting worse instead of better? Write out your perceptions of and feelings about the situation honestly.

Do you believe that God only goes forward? Do you believe that God, in response to prayer, moves situations in the direction of His will? Can you place your situation into this sentence and make it a faith-statement?

I know that God's will in _____ *is beneficial, pleasing, and fitting (Romans 12:1). I know, no matter what I may observe from the earth-perspective, that God is responding to my prayers and is moving* _____ *forward in the direction of His will. I know that He is merging this situation into His long-term plan. I know that His plan is to prosper and not to harm, to give a hope and a future (Jeremiah 29:11).*

❖

Dear reader, as you are taking hold of this faith-statement and making it yours, my prayer for you is found in Ephesians 1:18: "*I pray also that the eyes of your heart may be enlightened in order that you may **know**.*"

❖

Week 6, Day 2

PRACTICE A NEW WAY OF PRAYING

Thank God for every day of your wait, grounding your thanksgiving in His Word.

Be still before the LORD and wait patiently for him; do not fret when men succeed in their ways, when they carry out their evil schemes. —Psalm 37:7

DAY THREE

Today, look at another incident recorded in Scripture that will give us insight into God's activity during our waiting periods. Consider Hannah, mother of Samuel.

The account of Samuel's life begins with Hannah's yearning for a son, documented in the first chapter of 1 Samuel. The true story of Samuel, however, begins earlier. Hannah's prayer, we will discover, began in the heart of God.

Hannah is not the primary character in this story. Nor is Samuel. Pivotal to the whole story, the central cohesive element, the linchpin, is God Himself. Everything else—Hannah's barrenness, Hannah's prayer, Samuel's birth—is the working out of God's eternal agenda. Our first clear glimpse into what God is doing is found in 1 Samuel 3:1: *"In those days the word of the LORD was rare; there were not many visions."* What does this sentence tell us? It tells us that God had no one through whom to speak to His people. In the Old Covenant, God's messages to His people came through human messengers—priests or prophets. God entrusted His message to an individual, and that individual passed it on to the people. We see that God had no one whose heart was at His disposal; no one into whose heart He could pour His words.

Do you see how God has engaged Hannah and, by seeming to withhold her heart's desire, is really making her heart the reservoir of His own desire? God wants a prophet. Hannah wants a son.

God, as always, is working according to a plan. He is not at a loss. He says in 1 Samuel 2:35, *"I will raise up for myself a faithful priest, who will do according to what is in my heart and mind."* When Hannah found herself in this apparently hopeless situation, the truth was that God had a plan.

Now we've seen what God is doing, let's put Hannah into the picture. Chapter 1 of 1 Samuel describes the situation as it looks from earth. Hannah is longing for a son. Month after month, year after year, she mourns the son she isn't having. Hannah thinks the Lord has forgotten her, and the empirical evidence—the observable facts—would say that Hannah is right. The Scripture, in fact, says, *"The LORD had closed her womb"* (1 Samuel 1:5–6).

The turning point in Hannah's story comes in 1 Samuel 1:11. Hannah prays this prayer: *"O LORD Almighty, if you will only look upon your servant's misery and remember me, and not forget your servant but give her a son, then I will give him to the LORD for all the days of his life, and no razor will ever be used on his head."* Following this prayer, Hannah conceived and bore her long-awaited son, Samuel.

Note: The vow that a razor would never touch his head referred to the practice of the Nazarite sect. They refused to cut their hair lest a man-made instrument profane this God-given growth. Hannah's dedication of her son to the service of God is based on Numbers 6:1–21.

Why does this prayer seem to move God when her many prayers before seemed not to? Look at what the prayer says about the heart of Hannah.

First, it tells us that during the waiting period, God had focused her faith. I have to think that in the beginning of her marriage, Hannah assumed that the biological processes of her body would produce a son. Month after month, her confidence and trust in her body withered. By the time that Hannah prayed this prayer, she knew that only God could give her a son. Her faith was focused.

Next, it tells us that Hannah understood that if the Lord gave her a son, that son belonged to the Lord. From the beginning, Hannah had been ready to be the mother of a son. But she had not been ready to be the mother of a prophet. God intended for Hannah more than she could ask or think, and He had to prepare her heart to receive it. Hannah's heart and God's heart had to be a perfect match. During the prayer process, God fashioned in Hannah a heart like His. When Samuel was born, Hannah had her son and God had His prophet. *"The boy Samuel grew up in the presence of the LORD"* (1 Samuel 2:21).

When Samuel was born, Hannah's prayer was answered, but it was not the end of God's work. It was the beginning. Samuel became a priest, prophet, and judge in the nation of Israel. He was the fulfillment of God's vision—a faithful priest who will do what is in God's heart and mind. Samuel became such a strong intercessor for Israel that the Scripture says, *"Throughout Samuel's lifetime, the hand of the LORD was against the Philistines"* (1 Samuel 7:13). God's hand was against the enemies of Israel, not as long as they had a mighty warrior on the battlefield, but as long as they had a mighty warrior in the prayer closet.

Do you see the process of prayer? Before Hannah began to pray, God was at work laying the groundwork for His prophet. While Hannah was praying, God was at work preparing her for the answer He had in mind. After Hannah was through praying, God was at work through His servant Samuel, the answer to Hannah's prayer. When we're finished, God is just beginning.

Where do you see your own situation represented in Hannah's story?

Are you forgetting that God is the central and primary character in your story as He was in Hannah's?

What is God saying to you through Hannah's story?

Week 6, Day 3

PRACTICE A NEW WAY OF PRAYING

Thank God for every day of your wait, grounding your thanksgiving in His Word.

I wait for the LORD, my soul waits, and in his word I put my hope.
—Psalm 130:5

DAY FOUR

Let's revisit the story of Lazarus in John 11. Mary, Martha, and Lazarus were close friends of Jesus. He often spent time in their home. They knew Him as well as any person on earth knew Him. They had seen Him respond to needs over and over again. They knew what they could expect of Him, or so they thought.

When Lazarus became ill, Mary and Martha sent a message to Jesus. Their message was simple and represented their absolute faith in Jesus to respond to their needs. "Lord, the one you love is sick."

Observe what happens next. John, as he tells the story, sets the stage with these words: "*Now Jesus loved Martha and her sister and Lazarus*" (John 11:5 NASB). Why do you think he put that sentence in? I think it was because of what comes next. "*Now Jesus loved Martha and her sister and Lazarus. So when He heard that he was sick, He then stayed two days longer in the place where He was*" (John 11:5–6 NASB). John wanted to make it clear that when Jesus built a delay into the process, when He stayed two days longer in the place where He was, it was in the context of how much He loved Martha, Mary, and Lazarus.

We see the same principle at work in verses 14–15 when Jesus is talking with His disciples. "*Lazarus is dead, and I am glad **for your sakes** that I was not there, so that you may believe*" (NASB). Jesus said that the delay was profitable for His disciples. His delay, then, was loving, purposeful, profitable, and deliberate. It was necessary for accomplishing the bigger agenda He had in mind.

How did the delay benefit Mary, Martha, Lazarus, and the disciples? If Jesus had come to Bethany and healed Lazarus before he died, Mary's and Martha's prayer would have been answered. Their faith in Jesus would have been affirmed. They would have been more certain than ever that Jesus is Lord over illness. But they would never have known that Jesus is Lord over death. The Father is always teaching us the lordship of Jesus in deeper, more experiential ways. "Jesus is Lord" is the truth that anchors everything.

In Him the great clarification took place. When [the disciples] said, "Jesus is Lord," then everything in heaven and earth fell into place.
—E. Stanley Jones, *Mastery: The Art of Mastering Life*

God wanted to do more than they could think or imagine, and it required a waiting period. He wanted them to see the lordship of Jesus in areas that had never occurred to them before. That's how much He loved them.

We see something else in this story. God had a bigger plan, a more far-reaching plan, for how and when He wanted to heal Lazarus.

Imagine that Jesus had arrived at Bethany in time to heal Lazarus. Who would have seen His glory?

Read John 11:19. Why were Jews from the surrounding areas at Mary's and Martha's house? What did it take to bring them?

Read John 11:45. What happened because the Jews from the area had come to mourn Lazarus's death?

When it appears from earth that God is delaying, He is really putting pieces together that you had not thought of. He is engineering circumstances so that His power and glory will be on display. When God builds a waiting period into the course of your affairs, it means that what He is doing requires it. His apparent delays are loving, purposeful, and deliberate.

Week 6, Day 4

PRACTICE A NEW WAY OF PRAYING

Thank God for every day of your wait, grounding your thanksgiving in His Word.

I wait for you, O LORD; you will answer, O Lord my God. —Psalm 38:15

_____

_____

_____

_____

_____

DAY FIVE

In the praying life, God schedules waiting periods. The Word of God teaches that prayer—true prayer—is a long-term commitment. Jesus' teaching about prayer was, "*Keep on asking and it will be given you; keep on seeking and you will find; keep on knocking…and the door will be opened to you*" (Matthew 7:7 AMP). He teaches tenacity and perseverance. He told parables that illustrated persistent, persevering prayer. In one of His parables He described a widow who came to an unjust judge over and over again until she received what she needed. Luke introduces this parable with these words: "*Then Jesus told his disciples a parable to show them that they should always pray and not give up*" (Luke 18:1). The whole point of Jesus' parable was to teach us not to give up. Why did Jesus think it necessary to teach such a thing? Because He knew that prayer would require the kind of steadfastness and resolve that could, if misunderstood, make a person give up. He taught us that when we feel like giving up, we must not give in to it. Prayer is not for quitters.

Even though it appears sometimes that prayer isn't working, that God is delaying, the truth is that God is acting in fulfilled time. God does not act in elapsed time, but in fulfilled time. *"The time is fulfilled, and the kingdom of God is at hand"* (Mark 1:15 NASB). The word "fulfilled" means "filled full." God says, "I am filling your waiting period full. When I have filled it full—when I have done all that I need to do with it—your wait will be over and My kingdom will be revealed." Fulfilled time is measured by the readiness of the circumstances. When the time is ripe, when all the pieces have been put in place, God's answer will be revealed. His concern is not time, but timing. Everything has a ripe moment: *"There is a time for everything, and a season for every activity under heaven"* (Ecclesiastes 3:1).

God's timing is an astounding thing. He is a micromanager. Every detail is being worked into His plan to bring about His own ends. Think about, for example, all the details that had to fall in place with split-second timing for the infant Moses to be rescued from the Nile by the daughter of Pharaoh. Moses had to be rescued by the daughter of Pharaoh. God's plan was more than to save Moses' life; it was to put Moses in the very heart of Egyptian power and learning.

God's timing is an astounding thing. He is a micromanager. Every detail is being worked into His plan to bring about His own ends.

- It had to occur to Moses' mother to build an ark of bulrushes and set him afloat.
- Moses' mother had to set him afloat on the right day at the right time of day.
- The currents of the Nile had to be traveling in the right direction and at the right speed.
- Pharaoh's daughter had to be bathing in the Nile at the right time.
- Pharaoh's daughter had to be predisposed to desire an infant.
- The infant Moses had to cry at exactly the right moment.

And on and on we could go. Not one second, not one incident, was by chance. God is not "hoping for the best"; He is creating the best. Timing is everything. And God is a God of timing. Read the following excerpt from *Heart's Cry* for an illustration of fulfilled time.

There is much to be learned while waiting on God. God's apparent delays are not delays. God is always working. *"Jesus said to them, 'My Father is always at his work to this very day, and I, too, am working'"* **(John 5:17). He is always in the process of answering.**

Here is another illustration from my mothering experience. Stinson walks into the kitchen and says, "Mom, I'm ready for breakfast now." Before he asked me, I knew what I would fix him for breakfast. I had all the ingredients ready. I waited until he felt his need. Otherwise, he wouldn't eat the breakfast I prepared. When he asked me, I began to mix

the ingredients into a coffee cake, preheat the oven, pour the ingredients into a pan, place the pan in the oven, and set the timer. Stinson returns in a few minutes, which seems like "ages" in a child's perception.

"Mom, you said you'd fix my breakfast ages ago," he said.

"I did fix your breakfast," I reply.

"Well, I don't see it," he looked around.

"It's in the oven. When it's completely baked, I'll put it on the table for you to eat."

What looks like delay to the immature or uninformed is simply God in the process of answering. When the answer is ready to be revealed, it will be. God calls for persevering prayer. If Stinson had stayed in the kitchen with me, he would not have helped speed the process, but he would have seen the process. He would have had complete assurance that his breakfast was on the way. He would have been confident that the time for his breakfast to be set before him was settled.

Jesus taught that the kingdom of God works on the growth principle. There is always a process of revelation. In this process, there will be a period of no apparent progress. The Spirit-filled intercessor will recognize this as that stage of the process when the work of God is underground. Jesus tells this parable:

He also said, "This is what the kingdom of God is like. A man scatters seed on the ground. Night and day, whether he sleeps or gets up, the seed sprouts and grows, though he does not know how. All by itself the soil produces grain—first the stalk, then the head, then the full kernel in the head. As soon as the grain is ripe, he puts the sickle to it, because the harvest has come."
—Mark 4:26–29

The farmer plants the seed and provides the needed care. He doesn't worry about how that little seed will turn into an ear of corn. He simply pulls up the weeds and does all the maintenance required to allow the seed to grow. Your persevering prayer is not to change God's course, or wear Him down, but to provide the spiritual maintenance while God works through the process.

Another illustration from God's creation might be the incubation period during which a bird's fertilized egg reaches maturity and hatches a baby bird. Once a bird lays her eggs, she sits on them to incubate them. To the uninformed observer, it would appear that nothing is happening. That observer would be amazed if he knew just how much was happening. The incubating bird has tucked her eggs underneath her stomach feathers close to a bare spot called her brood patch. The brood patch is the warmest surface on the bird's body because of the network of blood vessels that lie close to the surface and produce heat. This heat is readily passed from the mother bird to her eggs. Her waiting is deliberate. The delay is essential to the outcome. All the work is invisible to the physical eye. As the mother sits on her eggs, the embryo is growing to a fully formed chick. When the chick is fully formed, it will hatch. When the time is fulfilled, the chicks will be revealed.

Our persevering intercession provides the incubating heat needed for our Spirit-born desires to reach maturity.

In summary, God has good, loving, and productive reasons for scheduling waiting periods into the prayer process. When He has called on you to wait, it is because what He is doing during the waiting time is necessary for the best outcome. If He didn't need the incubation time, it would not be there.

Week 6, Day 5

PRACTICE A NEW WAY OF PRAYING

Thank God for every day of your wait, grounding your thanksgiving in His Word.

But as for me, I watch in hope for the LORD, I wait for God my Savior; my God will hear me. —Micah 7:7

Week Six Anniversary Thought

When you are in God's waiting room, your spiritual vision is being developed. You have to look at the spiritual end of the spectrum. When you do, everything on earth will look different to you. Consider Joshua and Caleb:

God promised the nation of Israel a land flowing with milk and honey, a land that produced lush fruit and abundant grain. The land was called Canaan. As they reached the boundaries of Canaan after leaving Egypt, the Lord instructed Moses to send out a group of men to explore the land and bring back a report. It interests me that 12 men looked at the same scene, but they viewed it differently. All 12 spies actually brought back the same report. In essence, all of them agreed on the facts as follows: "The land is just exactly as God said it would be. It flows with milk and honey. Its fruit is large and its grain is lush. And there are giants in the land." They all agreed on the facts, but they interpreted the facts differently.

Ten of the men saw the negative: *"We went into the land to which you sent us, and it does flow with milk and honey! Here is its fruit. But the people who live there are powerful, and the cities are fortified and very large.... The land we explored devours those living in it. All the people we saw there are of great size.... We seemed like grasshoppers in our own eyes, and we looked the same to them"* (Numbers 13:27–28, 32–33).

Two of the men, Joshua and Caleb, had a different view. *"The land we passed through and explored is exceedingly good. If the LORD is pleased with us, he will lead us into that land, a land flowing with milk and honey, and will give it to us. Only do not rebel against the LORD. And do not be afraid of the people of the land, because we will swallow them up. Their protection is gone, but the LORD is with us. Do not be afraid of them"* (Numbers 14:7–9).

The 10 said, "We are grasshoppers in the eyes of our enemies!" Joshua and Caleb said, "Our enemies are grasshoppers in the eyes of the Lord!" The 10 said, "They will devour us!" Joshua and Caleb said, "We will swallow them up." The very same facts that caused fear in the 10, instead engaged faith in Caleb and Joshua. Caleb and Joshua saw an opportunity for God to act. They saw a platform for His power.

Spiritual vision will enable you to see everything in the light of **Jesus.** —from *Fueled by Faith*

Hearing from God

PRACTICE A NEW WAY OF PRAYING

This week as you pray, turn these promises into prayers. Ask God for what He longs to give—firsthand knowledge of Him.

DAY ONE

Hearing from God is the central work of prayer. During the prayer process, God is attuning our ears to His voice. Jesus said, *"My sheep listen to my voice …and they follow me"* (John 10:27). As a sheep learns to recognize the voice of its shepherd, so we learn to recognize the voice of our Shepherd. As we hear it over and over again, as we learn through experience to trust it, His voice becomes immediately familiar to us. This is a critical part of the prayer process.

Why do you think that hearing from God would be the central work of prayer?

Read the following statement from Jesus through carefully. Even if you know it by heart, read it through again, focusing on every phrase.

"I no longer call you servants, because a servant does not know his master's business. Instead, I have called you friends, for everything that I learned from my Father I have made known to you." —John 15:15

Now, circle these words in the verse: "because," "instead," and "for."

Read it back through, paying particular attention to the meaning these words point you toward. What are the implied truths here? For example, when Jesus says that He no longer calls you servant because a servant does not know his Master's business, does that not imply that you do know your Master's business?

The difference between being His slave and being His friend, Jesus taught, is that a friend will know His mind and heart. A friend will be privy to His intimate thoughts and longings.

Read John 16:14–15 and notice these points:

1. Everything that belongs to the Father belongs to Jesus. The Father's thoughts and desires belong to Jesus.

2. Everything that belongs to Jesus—the thoughts and desires of the Father, for example—are delivered to you by the Holy Spirit. They become yours.

Reread John 16:15. What will Jesus make known to you?

The Father speaks through the Son; the Son speaks through the Spirit. *From* the Father, *through* the Son, *by* the Spirit—this is how God speaks to you and to me.

Scripture is filled with invitations to listen to God. Would God instruct you to do something that it was impossible for you to do? Since God tells you to listen to Him, since He promises you that He will instruct and teach you, is not the implied promise that you can hear Him?

Read the following Scriptures and rewrite them in the first person. (Instead of "Whether you turn..." write "Whether I turn....")

Isaiah 30:21

Psalm 25:12

Psalm 32:8

John 10:27

In Hebrews 4:7 we read: *"Today, if you hear his voice, do not harden your hearts."* The word translated "hear" means "to hear and respond in one action." This seems to teach us that responding is the key to clear hearing. If I hear His voice and do not respond, a callous begins to form over my heart. It begins to harden. The next time He speaks, it's harder for me to hear Him. His voice is less distinct. Disobedience by disobedience, my heart becomes more calloused and less able to discern His voice. However, the opposite is also true. If I hear and do respond, the callous over my heart begins to slough away. The next time He speaks, it is easier for me to hear. Obedience by obedience, my heart softens and I become more astute at hearing His voice.

What have you heard the Lord say to you to which you have not responded? What do you keep pushing to the background of your life, but the Lord's voice keeps bringing it back to the surface? Has that voice grown fainter since you first heard it? Respond to what the Lord is telling you right now. Write it down.

Week 7, Day 1

PRACTICE A NEW WAY OF PRAYING

Harvest this promise by asking God for what He longs to give. Turn His promise into a prayer.

Who, then, is the man that fears the LORD? He will instruct him in the way chosen for him. —Psalm 25:12

_____

_____

_____

_____

_____

_____

DAY TWO

We must be able to hear from God because He alone is the source of true prayer. His desires pour into our hearts so that they become our desires and are expressed through our words—this is the goal of the praying life. He promises to pour out His heart and to make His thoughts known to us (Proverbs 1:23). Hannah Hurnard writes, "Prayer is essentially the contact of our minds with the mind of God, resulting in real conversation with Him."

In order to develop confidence in our ability to hear from God, we must first accept that we *can* hear from God—that God has made it possible. He speaks to us from within, from His dwelling place in our spirit-center. Here He has made His home. He is not speaking to us from a faraway place. He is speaking into our thoughts, into our emotions, into our wills. He is speaking so intimately that many times it feels like our own ideas. But as He has more and more access to us, He is able to think His thoughts in us. It is His indwelling Life that makes it possible for us to hear Him moment by moment.

Not from without but from within, not in word but in power, in life and truth, the Spirit reveals Christ and all He has for us. He makes the Christ, who has been to us so much only an image, a thought, a Saviour outside and above us, to be truth within us. The Spirit brings the truth into us; and then, having possessed us from within, guides us, as we can bear it, into all the truth. —Andrew Murray, *The Spirit of Christ*

[At Pentecost] they were not submerged in God, nor did God override them. God was God and they were they; but Person flowed into person, Will into will, Mind into mind, and they could scarcely tell where they ended and God began. He was closer than the blood in their veins and nearer than their own heartbeats. If they should reach out to touch Him, they would reach too far.
—E. Stanley Jones, *Mastery: The Art of Mastering Life*

Man willingly becomes the channel for the yearnings of God's heart.
—R. Arthur Mathews, *Born for Battle*

On the first day of Pentecost He returned, not this time to be with them externally...but now to be in them, imparting to them His own divine nature, clothing Himself with their humanity...He spoke with their lips, He worked with their hands. This was the miracle of the new birth, and this remains the very heart of the gospel!
—Major Ian Thomas, *The Saving Life of Christ*

In learning to hear God's present voice, you don't have to worry about whether you are good at hearing. You can trust that He is good at speaking.

It is critical, as we look carefully at how God speaks to believers today, to get it clearly in our minds that God—God the Father, God the Son, and God the Spirit—indwells us. Some have the impression that a watered-down, shadow-version of God called "the Spirit" indwells us and that God and Jesus live in a faraway land called heaven. Not so. God is One. He is not fragmented. Everything God does and everything He says, He does and says as the Triune God: from the Father, through the Son, by the Spirit.

Read John 14:23. Who is "we"?

Where will the Father and the Son abide?

> *In learning to hear God's present voice, you don't have to worry about whether you are good at hearing. You can trust that He is good at speaking.*

Read 1 Corinthians 3:16. Whose temple (dwelling place) are you?

Read 1 Corinthians 6:19. Whose temple (dwelling place) are you?

Think about this sentence from Jesus' high priestly prayer: "I (Jesus) in them (believers) and you (the Father) in me (Jesus)" (John 17:23).

Where is Jesus?

Where is God?

Triune God: The Lord Our God Is One

Let me try to illustrate the oneness of the Father, the Son, and the Spirit in Their communication to you. Imagine that I have the most wonderful thoughts and that if you only knew my thoughts, your life would be changed forever. What would I have to do? I would have to translate my thoughts into words. Then my words would be the exact representation of my thoughts. My words would be my thoughts in a different form. The essence of my words and my thoughts would be exactly the same, but my thoughts would now be in the form of words.

It will take one more element for me to be able to get my thoughts across to you. It will take the breath of my mouth rushing over my vocal chords to form the voice that makes my words heard. My voice takes my words and makes them known to you.

Do you see how I speak *from* my thoughts, *through* my words, *by* my voice? Three actions in one.

Let my thoughts represent the Father, whose thoughts toward you are wonderful and precious according to Psalm 139:17–18; whose thoughts are higher than your thoughts according to Isaiah 55:8–9. The Father translated Himself into Word, according to John 1:1. Just as my thoughts are my words, so the Word was God. God the Father and God the Son are the same essence in different forms. The Thought was now in the form of Word (John 1:1–2, 14). The Word is the exact representation of the Thought (Hebrews 1:3). The Word makes the Thought known (John 1:18).

Now the third element: the Spirit. The Greek word *pneuma*, translated "Spirit," is also translated "breath." The Breath of God's mouth is a picture of the Holy Spirit throughout the Old Testament (Job 33:4; Ezekiel 37:9). Just as my breath creates the voice that delivers my words, the Spirit takes Jesus and makes Him known to you (John 16:15). *From* the Father, *through* the Son, *by* the Spirit.

He is speaking from within you. Turn inward to Him and His indwelling life. Listen to the voice that now lives in you. You need not search for God. He has made you His abode. As E. Stanley Jones said, if you reach out for Him, you have reached too far.

❖

Week 7, Day 2

PRACTICE A NEW WAY OF PRAYING

Harvest this promise by asking God for what He longs to give. Turn His promise into a prayer.

We have not received the spirit of the world but the Spirit who is from God, that we may understand what God has freely given us. —1 Corinthians 2:12

DAY THREE

God has always been and will always be a speaking God. He is forever speaking His power onto the earth. God says, "Let there be…" and it is so.

God's Word Working

God does His work by His Word. When God speaks, His Word is the instrument of His work.

"As the rain and the snow come down from heaven, and do not return to it without watering the earth and making it bud and flourish, so that it yields seed for the sower and bread for the eater, so is my word that goes out from my mouth: It will not return to me empty, but will accomplish what I desire and achieve the purpose for which I sent it." —Isaiah 55:10–11

Do you see how God talks about His Word? He says that He sends His Word out with an assignment and that His Word always accomplishes His desires and achieves His purposes. His Word accomplishes His work. His Word waters and nourishes the lives into which He sends it and makes them bud and flourish. He always does His work by His Word.

By the word of the LORD were the heavens made, their starry host by the breath of his mouth.…For he spoke, and it came to be; he commanded, and it stood firm. —Psalm 33:6, 9

Jesus once said, *"The **words** I say to you are not just my own. Rather, it is the Father, living in me, who is doing his **work**"* (John 14:10). Jesus said that the words He was speaking were doing the Father's work. Why? Because they were the Father's words! The Father's words do the Father's work.

In the same passage, Jesus continued by saying, *"Believe me when I say that I am in the Father and the Father is in me; or at least believe on the evidence of the miracles themselves"* (John 14:11). Here's what Jesus was saying: **The Father's words, which I am speaking, are doing the Father's miracles. Here's the proof that the Father is in Me: His words coming through Me are doing His works.**

God's words are different from your words or my words. In the material realm, words have no substance. They do not have mass and take up space. They are puffs of air. Earth words communicate, but they do not accomplish work. I can't say to an object, "Move from here to there," and expect the object to move. I have to use physical force to move an earth object from one place to another. My words do not do my work.

The Father's words are different. In the spiritual realm, God's words have substance. They are not puffs of air; they are the instruments of His action. *"God said, 'Let there be light,' and there was light"* (Genesis 1:3). He created the earth by His Word. He is watching over His Word to see that it is carried out.

He is still doing His work by His Word. He is still speaking His creating, sustaining, and ruling Word. He is speaking through the Son, by the Spirit, to you and to me.

Clearly understanding that Jesus' life is flowing through you and operating in you is essential for understanding everything else about prayer. His life is the underlying reality, the ground from which every prayer principle grows.

Jesus taught us that His Spirit-life in us would be superior to His physical presence with us. He said to His disciples, who had grown dependent upon His earthly presence, *"I tell you the truth:* **It is for your good** *that I am going away. Unless I go away, the Counselor will not come to you; but if I go, I will send him to you"* (John 16:7). Jesus said that His life indwelling us in Spirit-form would be to our benefit. Why? Because from within, Jesus Himself would speak directly into our understanding. We can hear Him more clearly than the disciples could hear Him when He was on earth in physical form. We can hear with understanding. We can hear His *rhema*, His present-tense speaking, all the time. He never leaves us. This form of hearing—hearing from within, Spirit-voice to Spirit-ears—is superior to hearing with our earth ears. Spirit-hearing is more reliable than earth hearing. Jesus said it is for our benefit that He has made His Spirit-life available and has removed His physical presence.

Depend on His life flowing through you right now. Depend on His Spirit-voice speaking to your understanding. Any understanding about spiritual truth that you acquire comes directly from Him. He may use a tool—a teacher, a writer, a preacher—but that person is a tool, not a source. He is the one and only source of spiritual understanding. Trust Him. He speaks by opening your mind so that you can understand the Scripture. (See Luke 24:45.)

What is God's purpose for speaking to you? What assurance does this give you that He wants you to be able to hear Him?

We are all insecure about our ability to hear the voice of God. We are all careful to ask, "Is it God, or is it me?" Don't trust your ability to hear.

Trust His ability to speak. He will take all the responsibility if you and I will open our lives to His voice.

The Sovereign LORD has given me an instructed tongue, to know the word that sustains the weary. He wakens me morning by morning, wakens my ear to listen like one being taught. The Sovereign LORD has opened my ears, and I have not been rebellious; I have not drawn back. —Isaiah 50:4–5

What do you think is meant by "an instructed tongue"?
(Read 1 Corinthians 2:13 and Luke 12:12 for clarification.)

What does a person with an instructed tongue know?

If a word has the power to hold up the weary, whose word must it be?

A person who is speaking with an instructed tongue is speaking whose word?

From where does an instructed tongue come?

How does God give an instructed tongue?

Who opens the ears and makes the learner able to "listen like one being taught"?

What is the hearer's responsibility?

Week 7, Day 3

<u>PRACTICE A NEW WAY OF PRAYING</u>

Harvest this promise by asking God for what He longs to give. Turn His promise into a prayer.

My purpose is that they may be encouraged in heart and united in love, so that they may have the full riches of complete understanding, in order that they may know the mystery of God, namely, Christ. —Colossians 2:2

DAY FOUR

God makes it clear that He cannot be fully known from any outside source. During the time that the Old Covenant was in effect, God spoke to His people through outside sources. He spoke through prophets and priests, He spoke through Ten Commandments written on tablets of stone, He led His people through the desert in fire by night and cloud by day—outside sources. Now we have a New Covenant, *"a better covenant, which was established upon better promises"* (Hebrews 8:6 KJV). In the New Covenant, God Himself speaks to each of His children from inside, through His indwelling presence. *"In the past God spoke to our forefathers through the prophets at many times and in various ways, but in these last days he has spoken to us by his Son"* (Hebrews 1:1–2). Everything that had been outside would now be inside.

"The time is coming, declares the Lord, when I will make a new covenant with the house of Israel and with the house of Judah. It will not be like the covenant I made with their forefathers when I took them by the hand to lead them out of Egypt...This is the covenant I will make with the house of Israel after that time, declares the Lord. I will put my laws in their minds and write them on their hearts. I will be their God, and they will be my people. No longer will a man teach his neighbor, or a man his brother, saying, 'Know the Lord,' because they will all know me, from the least of them to the greatest." —Hebrews 8:8–11

Do you see how the Scripture contrasts the two covenants? In the first, God's words were outside, guiding; in the second, God's Word is inside, transforming. In 1 John 2:27, we read that the Father has given you an anointing that lives in you. The "anointing" is the Spirit's presence in power. Because of the indwelling life of God, you can know truth. (We'll look at this verse from 1 John more carefully further on.)

Information from an outside source may be true, but it can't reach the understanding without being distorted. Have you ever made a comment to someone, or passed on information to someone, and by the time it reached that person's understanding it was different from what you had said? The person heard your words, but misunderstood your meaning. Let me illustrate how unreliable information from an outside source can be, even if it's true. My niece Hannah was about 3 years old when Hurricane Andrew hit Florida. Hannah lives in Houston. The weather reports warned that the hurricane might be headed for Houston. My sister Julie said to Hannah, "We have to go to the grocery store and get some food because a hurricane's coming."

Hannah asked, "What's a hurricane?"

Julie replied, "It's a big storm and it rains and it blows..."

Hannah said, "And it eats?"

Information, which comes from an outside source, always has to be filtered through worldview, mind-set, knowledge of the subject, preconceived ideas, and on and on. Information, no matter what form it started out in, never reaches the understanding undistorted. When God spoke to His people through outside sources, He spoke only truth, but it reached their understanding in a distorted form.

When God speaks to you from within, He is acting directly on your understanding. The word Scripture uses to describe the direct action of God on your mind and understanding is "revelation." What does the Scripture mean by "revelation"?

In order to see this concept very clearly, we're going to take it apart and put it back together again. First, I want you to see what it means to have the Spirit's indwelling and to be filled with the Spirit.

The Scripture describes man as a three-in-one being, made in the image of the three-in-one God.

1. Man is packaged in a body (Greek: *soma*), which is made of earth-substance. It is through the body that man relates to and interacts with his physical environment.
2. Man has a soul (Greek: *psuche*). His soul is his mind, will, and emotions. His soul is his human nature. Through the soul, humans relate to each other and to thoughts and ideas.
3. Man is spirit (Greek: *pneuma*). It is through his spirit that he relates to God.

The writer of Hebrews, for example, says that the Word of God will divide between *soul* and *spirit* (Hebrews 4:12). Paul prays, "*May God himself, the*

*God of peace, sanctify you through and through. May your whole **spirit**, **soul** and **body** be kept blameless at the coming of our Lord Jesus Christ"* (1 Thessalonians 5:23). Although the words "soul" and "spirit" are often used interchangeably to indicate the inner man, Scripture makes clear that body, soul, and spirit are three distinct aspects of man. Let the following illustration picture for you man as three-in-one.

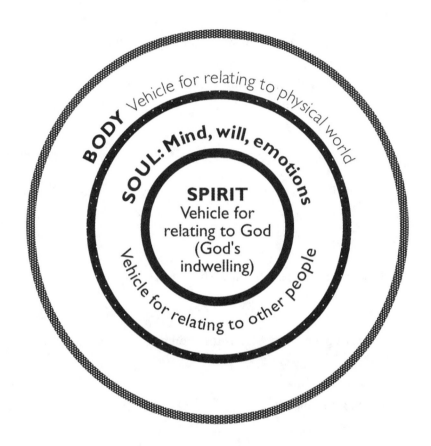

It is in your spirit-center that God indwells you. That is where His Holy of Holies is.

From your spirit, God's dwelling place, God expresses Himself through your mind (Romans 12:2), will (Philippians 2:13), and emotions (Romans 5:5)—your soul. Your soul is pictured by the Holy Place in the temple—the place where the activities of worship were carried out.

Through your body, God works in the world. Your body is the physical vehicle through which your inner man—spirit and soul—is expressed. Your body would correspond to the outer courtyard of the temple, which was the part of the temple visible to all.

To be filled with the Spirit means to have your soul and your body—your thinking, feeling, willing, and acting—under the authority of His indwelling Spirit.

If God—all of God: the Father, Son, and Spirit—indwells you, then all of Truth indwells you. Truth is living in your spirit because Truth is a person. All of God is in Jesus; all of Jesus is in the Spirit; all of the Spirit is in you.

"No longer will a man teach his neighbor, or a man his brother, saying, 'Know the Lord,' because they will all know me, from the least of them to the greatest." —Hebrews 8:11

As for you, the anointing you received from him remains in you, and you do not need anyone to teach you. But as his anointing teaches you about all things and as that anointing is real, not counterfeit—just as it has taught you, remain in him. —1 John 2:27

Look at Hebrews 8:11. Under the New Covenant, why will man not have to teach his brother or his neighbor to know the Lord?

Why will all His people know Him?

Look at 1 John 2:27. What is the anointing?

Where is the anointing?

Where did the anointing come from?

What does the anointing do?

All truth is indwelling your spirit-center. Truth is abiding in you. But your *mind* does not have all truth. Not all truth is in your understanding.

Where is your mind and your intellect? It is in your soul, not your spirit.

Now, go back with me to the word "revelation." It means "unveiling or uncovering." The Scripture says that a veil lies over our minds that is only removed by Jesus Christ (2 Corinthians 3:16). The truth in your spirit is progressively being unveiled to your mind (understanding) by Jesus Himself. He is continually lifting the veil that hides deep truth so that you see and comprehend more and more of His Word each day. Just as He did for the disciples, Jesus is opening your mind so that you can understand the Scripture (Luke 24:45). God is giving you a spirit of wisdom and revelation so that you will know Him better (Ephesians 3:17–19).

God has many ways in which He unveils truth to our minds. For one thing, He has appointed and gifted tools in the Body through whom He unveils truth. Those who have the gift of teaching or preaching or prophecy are often the mouthpieces He uses, but they are not the source. God is the only one who can bring understanding of spiritual truth to your mind. Truth comes *from* the spirit *to* the mind.

<u>PRACTICE A NEW WAY OF PRAYING</u>

Harvest this promise by asking God for what He longs to give. Turn His promise into a prayer.

For this reason, since the day we heard about you, we have not stopped praying for you and asking God to fill you with the knowledge of his will through all spiritual wisdom and understanding. —Colossians 1:9

DAY FIVE

God speaks by revealing the truth in His Word at progressively deeper levels. Only He can do that. No matter how wonderful you may think a speaker or writer is, he or she cannot reveal truth to your understanding. If someone's words have produced new insight in you, it is because God Himself has revealed it. Information comes from outside sources. Revelation comes from God within you.

First Corinthians 2:9–16 shows the difference between information *about* God and revelation *from* God. We see that God reveals to our understanding that which is freely available to us. We speak what we understand. We speak spiritual words—words that are taught us by the Spirit Himself.

No eye has seen, no ear has heard, no mind has conceived what God has prepared for those who love him… (v. 9)

God has things prepared for us—things that are ready and waiting for our use. We cannot know these things in the same way we know what exists on the earth. We can't know God's provision by seeing or hearing or imagining.

…but God has revealed it to us by his Spirit. (v. 10)

What we cannot know by seeing, hearing, or imagining, we can know by the Spirit's revelation. The word "revelation" means uncovering or unveiling. The Spirit unveils God's truths to our understanding. When the Spirit brings understanding, we will know what God has ready and waiting as certainly as if we'd seen them with our eyes or heard them with our ears.

The Spirit searches all things, even the deep things of God. (v. 10)

When we are depending on the Spirit to bring understanding of spiritual truth, we will have access to even the deep, mysterious, hidden things that belong to God. See Daniel 2:22.

For who among men knows the thoughts of a man except the man's spirit within him? (v. 11)

No one knows me but me. No one knows my thoughts but my spirit within me. If you want to know what I think, I will have to reveal my thoughts to you.

In the same way, no one knows the thoughts of God except the Spirit of God. (v. 11)

Just like no one knows me but me, no one knows God but God. If you want to know His thoughts, He will have to reveal them to you.

We have not received the spirit of the world but the Spirit who is from God, that we may understand what God has freely given us. (v. 12)

God has revealed Himself to us. He has given us His Spirit. He has given us Himself. The purpose for giving us His Spirit is so that we can understand what He has prepared for us and has made freely available to us.

This is what we speak, not in words taught us by human wisdom but in words taught by the Spirit, expressing spiritual truths in spiritual words. (v. 13)

What do we speak? We speak what we understand. What does God's Spirit cause us to understand? From the Spirit, we understand what God has freely given us. If God Himself has revealed truth into our understanding, when we speak that understanding, we are speaking spiritual words. What makes them spiritual? They are born of the Spirit. Whatever is born of the Spirit is spirit. We can now say, "These words I speak, they are spirit and they are life."

In prayer, we speak the things that we know by the Spirit to be freely available to us. These words are spirit and life. They are God's words. God's words do exactly what God has assigned them to do. They are settled forever in the heavens. God's words do God's work.

When I speak God's words on earth, they impact the spiritual realm. The spiritual realm impacts the material realm. The life of Jesus flowing through me continually is creating my thoughts, desires, imaginings, and will, and is authoring in me the Spirit-born word of God.

God wants you to hear Him. He has put everything in place so that you and I will be able to hear Him speaking in the present tense. He speaks from within directly into our understanding. Many times, what the Lord wants to say He has already deposited in your mind and you find it pouring out through your mouth as prayer.

Indeed the whole secret of prayer is found in these three words, in the Spirit. It is the prayer that God the Holy Spirit inspires that God the Father answers. —R. A. Torrey, *How to Pray*

There are times when prayer pours forth in volumes and originality such as we cannot create. It rolls through us like a mighty tide. Our prayers are mingled with a vaster Word, a Word that at one time was made flesh. We pray, and yet it is not we who pray, but a Greater who prays in us.... All we can say is, Prayer is taking place, and I am given to be in the orbit. —Thomas Kelly, *A Testament of Devotion*

I seek in myself the things I hoped to say,
But lo! my wells are dry.
Then, seeing me empty, you forsake
The listener's role and through
My dumb lips breathe and into utterance wake
The thoughts I never knew.
—C. S. Lewis, quoted in *Letters to Malcolm*

Week 7, Day 5

PRACTICE A NEW WAY OF PRAYING

Harvest this promise by asking God for what He longs to give. Turn His promise into a prayer.

Thou hast given me an open ear. —Psalm 40:6 (RSV)

He... wakens my ear to listen like one being taught. The Sovereign Lord *has opened my ears.* —Isaiah 50:4–5

Week Seven Anniversary Thought

The person of Jesus embodies fully the Word of God. He is the Word. He is the living Word that the written word conveys. If there were no Living Word, then there would be no written word to express Him. Without the eternal Living Word, there would be no word to be spoken. Because He is, therefore everything that exists is. *"Without him nothing was made that has been made"* (John 1:3). The writer of Hebrews refers to the Son *"through whom he made the universe"* (Hebrews 1:2). Paul describes Him this way: *"By him all things were created: things in heaven and on earth, visible and invisible, whether thrones or powers or rulers or authorities; all things were created by him and for him. He is before all things, and in him all things hold together"* (Colossians 1:16–17).

The Word has always been. The Word is. The Word will always be. And the Word lives in you. *"The word is near you; it is in your mouth and in your heart"* (Romans 10:8).

When you read the written Word, the Living Word speaks it to you. He speaks to you in present and specific ways, heart to heart. He presents His thoughts to your mind in a fashion that is tailored to your personality and experiences. For example, my friend Libby is an artist. Jesus speaks often to her through colors because she thinks a lot about colors. My friend Mary is a master gardener, and Jesus speaks often to her in gardening metaphors because she knows a lot about gardening. I am a left-brained logical person and Jesus speaks to me in logic and thought sequences. For all of us, He is right there in our present moment speaking life-altering truth in a direct transfer from His mind to ours. Why can He do that? Because *"we have the mind of Christ"* (1 Corinthians 2:16). We have Jesus' thoughts in a present state—as He thinks them right now—as they are relevant to your moment and to your life.

Jesus is the Word of God. He is always speaking to you from within. He speaks the Scripture into a present reality. He speaks personal and specific words of promise to you. He creates in you the desires of God for you. *"For it is God who works* in you *to will and to act according to his good purpose"* (Philippians 2:13, emphasis mine).

Jesus, when He lived in His physical body on earth, was the container for God's words and the vehicle for their expression. He is the Living

Word. Where does Jesus now abide? Are you seeing that you can't separate the Living Word from the written Word? It is the Living Word who infuses the Scripture with Spirit and life.

Seeking After God

This week, concentrate your prayer time on opening your life to God and seeking Him. Let each day's thought guide you to His heart.

DAY ONE

The third part of the prayer process is seeking after God. The irony is that when we begin seeking God, it is only because He is seeking us. It is His pull on our hearts that causes us to desire Him. Without His initiative, we would never seek Him out. *"There is no one who understands, no one who seeks God"* (Romans 3:11). He could not have put it in stronger terms—*no one* has in himself the understanding that would cause him to seek God. When we find within ourselves the initiative to seek God, it is really a response to His invitation to seek Him. *"When You said, 'Seek My face,' my heart said to You, 'Your face, O Lord, I shall seek'"* (Psalm 27:8 NASB).

"'You will seek me and find me when you seek me with all your heart. I will be found by you,' declares the Lord" (Jeremiah 29:13–14). Look carefully at what He says. When you seek Him—respond to His pull on your heart—you will, without a doubt, find Him. He has made Himself "find-able." He says, "I will be found by you." He makes Himself the subject—the doer of the action. He will *do* the "being found."

The Book of Hebrews tells us that God *"rewards those who earnestly seek him"* (Hebrews 11:6). The reward of a search is finding that for which you are searching. For example, a person who is searching for sunken treasure would feel himself rewarded by finding sunken treasure. God rewards those who seek Him. What is that reward? Himself. God said to Abraham, *"I am...your very great reward"* (Genesis 15:1). When He Himself is the focal point of our search—not blessings by way of Him, but *Him*—we are extravagantly, exorbitantly rewarded. When we find Him, we find everything. Julian of Norwich prayed, "God, of Your goodness, give me Yourself; for You are sufficient for me. I cannot properly ask anything less to be worthy of You. If I were to ask less, I should always be in want. In You alone do I have all."

Read the following statements Scripture makes about the aggressive love of the Father. See how He is characterized as the initiator, seeking us out. Write out what each passage says to you about God's activity toward you.

Romans 10:20

Luke 19:10

John 4:23

Take the time in His presence to let the truth soak in—every desire you feel toward God is proof that He is seeking you and seeking your presence with Him. Write out your response to His reaching, seeking love.

We seek God through the spiritual disciplines. By engaging in the spiritual disciplines, we keep our lives open to God so that He can do in us and through us what He desires. He can fulfill His purposes in us when we are accessible to Him.

The plans of the LORD stand firm forever, the purposes of his heart through all generations. —Psalm 33:11

I cry out to God Most High, to God, who fulfills his purpose for me. —Psalm 57:2

The LORD will fulfill his purpose for me; your love, O LORD, endures forever—do not abandon the works of your hands. —Psalm 138:8

We do not need more access to God. Full access was provided through the finished work of Christ. *"Therefore, brothers, since we have confidence to enter the Most Holy Place by the blood of Jesus, by a new and living way opened for us through the curtain, that is, his body, and since we have a great priest over the house of God, let us draw near to God with a sincere heart in full assurance of faith, having our hearts sprinkled to cleanse us from a guilty conscience and having our bodies washed with pure water"* (Hebrews 10:19–22).

God needs access to us. He waits for us to open the door to His Son. *"Here I am! I stand at the door and knock. If anyone hears my voice and opens the door, I will come in and eat with him, and he with me"* (Revelation 3:20). Always, the Son is knocking, seeking entrance to our lives and to our needs. Always, His word is, "Here I am!" Engaging in the spiritual disciplines is one way we open our lives to Him and to all He wants to do.

Engaging in the disciplines does not earn us favor with God. We don't engage in the disciplines because God will then be moved to do good for us. The spiritual disciplines accomplish only one thing: they are our "yes" to God's invitation.

Week 8, Day 1

PRACTICE A NEW WAY OF PRAYING

Let this thought guide your prayer time today. Journal your prayer.

My goal is God Himself, not joy, nor peace,
        Nor even blessing, but Himself, my God;
'Tis His to lead me there, not mine, but His—
        "At any cost, dear Lord, by any road."
—F. Bruce; quoted from *Christian Disciplines* by Oswald Chambers

_____

_____

_____

_____

_____

DAY TWO

God has designed it so that He can speak to His children through the Bible. The Bible is much more than the words God once spoke; it is the Word He is now speaking. Every word written in the Scripture is from God, and God Himself has watched over, protected, and preserved His Word since the beginning.

Don't fall into the habit of thinking of the Bible as an ordinary book. It is far more! As you are reading the Word of God, God's Spirit is speaking it to you in terms of your life. He is causing you to understand it and to see its truth.

But to the soul born from above, the Bible is the universe of God's revealed will.... The stupendous profundities of God's will, surging

with unfathomable mysteries, come down to the shores of our common life, not in emotions and fires, nor in aspirations and vows, agonies and visions, but in a way so simple that wayfaring men, though fools, cannot make a mistake, that is, in words....

As soon as any soul is born from above, the Bible becomes to him the universe of revelation facts, just as the natural world is the universe of common-sense facts....God's Spirit speaks an understanding of His Word never known before....God's sayings are sealed to every soul until they are opened by the indwelling Spirit of God.
—Oswald Chambers, *Christian Disciplines*

To help us understand the value of His Word, God has represented His Word as food that nourishes our spiritual life in the same way that physical food nourishes our physical life.

Read the following Scripture references. What does God want you to see about His Word from each of these statements?

Matthew 4:4

Psalm 119:103–104

Jeremiah 15:16

Ezekiel 3:1–4

Just as my body requires a daily, consistent intake of food, my spirit requires a daily, consistent intake of God's Word. I need to be engaged in the discipline of continually ingesting spiritual nourishment so that I will progressively mature and so that my spiritual immune system will be strong.

Through a consistent daily intake of God's Word, God will reveal His heart and mold our prayers. Let's compare eating food in the physical realm and taking in the Word in the spiritual realm.

Physically, when you eat food, the nutrients from that food are absorbed into your bloodstream to be delivered to your cells. How do the right nutrients reach the right cells? How does protein get to your muscle cells and calcium to your bone cells? Why don't nutrients get deposited in the wrong cells? Our food all enters our bodies the same way, and yet the specific nutrients and vitamins get to the right cells.

The reason is that an amazingly complex system clicks "on" when you eat food. It's called your digestive system. The first stage of digestion is changing food into a form the body can use. The second is delivering the food to the cells. The nutrients and vitamins are absorbed into the bloodstream and the bloodstream is the delivery system. Every cell has its own specifically designed receptor sites that are shaped so that they match the shape of the nutrient that cell requires. The receptor site attracts out of your bloodstream exactly what it needs.

Amazing, isn't it? You have billions of cells in your body, each drawing out of your bloodstream exactly what it needs. This complicated and complex process happens without your effort. You don't even have to know what happens or how it happens for it to happen. You don't have to feel it happening. You just have to eat the food; your body does the rest. The nutrients in your food literally are *"life to those who find them and health to a man's whole body,"* which is exactly how Proverbs 4:20–22 describes the Word of God. Once your food and its nutrients enter your body, they become *"living and active,"* as the writer of Hebrews tells us the Word of God is (Hebrews 4:12).

Nourishing your spirit works the same way. You feast on the Word of God and God Himself applies His truth to your life. His Word is not alive and active written on a page and bound in a book. His Word comes to life in you when it comes into contact with your faith (Hebrews 4:2). When you take in the Word, the Spirit of God in you breathes life into it. He reveals its truth. He opens your mind to understand. When you engage in the discipline of taking in the Word of God on a regular basis, your spiritual digestive system does the rest.

Nourishing your spirit works the same way. You feast on the Word of God and God Himself applies His truth to your life.

What would happen if you did not eat the foods that contain the nutrients your body needs? Your cells would have no nutrients to draw from your bloodstream. Your bloodstream only has available the nutrients you have ingested. If you don't take in the Word of God, your spirit has no nourishment from which to draw. The Spirit of God can only make alive the Word of God that you have taken in. The writer of Hebrews compares Scripture to food in an interesting way.

We have much to say about this, but it is hard to explain because you are slow to learn. In fact, though by this time you ought to be teachers, you need someone to teach you the elementary truths of God's word all over again. You need milk, not solid food! Anyone who lives on milk, being still an infant, is not acquainted with the teaching about righteousness. But solid food is for the mature, who by constant use have trained themselves to distinguish good from evil. —Hebrews 5:11–14

The writer of Hebrews says that the same Scripture is received as "milk" by some and as "meat" by others. Some believers, it seems, have not eaten enough of the Word to develop a mature digestive system. They can only access what they can skim off the surface. Others, though, have eaten enough spiritual food that their spiritual digestive system can metabolize meat. They can access the deeper, more substantive truths in God's Word. How have they reached this maturity? Hebrews explains it this way: "*who **by constant use** have trained themselves.*" These believers have constantly used the Word. The word translated *use* means "exercise or practice." Those who mature to deeper levels of the truth are those who put the Word to use in their lives. God speaks not to inform, but to transform. God's Word is not designed to lie passive and untried in our lives. God's Word has muscle power!

Do you want to move on from milk to meat? Make constant use of the Word you know.

How are you to use the Word of God? Look up the following Scripture references for clarification.

Psalm 119:9

Psalm 119: 59–60

Proverbs 6:23

Ephesians 6:17

To let the Word of God come to life in us, we must be engaged in an ongoing daily discipline of Bible study. We must look for every possible way to ingest His Word. We will not hear Him clearly if we look for His communication only for certain times in certain circumstances. Our lives are to be a repository of His Word where we store it up and have it ready for His use at any given moment. He speaks to us through His Word as part of the prayer process.

We must approach our Bible study listening for Him, whatever He would say, not listening for what we want Him to say. Let Habakkuk be a model for us: "*I will stand on my guard post and station myself on the rampart; and I will keep watch to see what He will speak to me, and how I may reply when I am reproved*" (Habakkuk 2:1 NASB). Habakkuk, when he needed to hear from God, stationed himself on a high tower at his guard post. This is the picture of an intercessor used throughout the Old Testament. He took himself away, removed himself from the fray for a moment.

He got up high—got perspective. What is the first thing Habakkuk does? He watches to see what God will say.

The danger is that we will try to put words in God's mouth. Too often we come to Him expecting Him to validate our decisions, and so miss Him altogether. Many times what He says will redefine our problem—help us see it as His opportunity to show His power. But when we are listening for what we want to hear instead of what He wants to say, we will miss Him. We must come to Him without preconceived ideas of what He will say. Ask Him to open your ear *"to listen like one being taught"* (Isaiah 50:4).

Week 8, Day 2

PRACTICE A NEW WAY OF PRAYING

Let this thought guide your prayer time today. Journal your prayer.

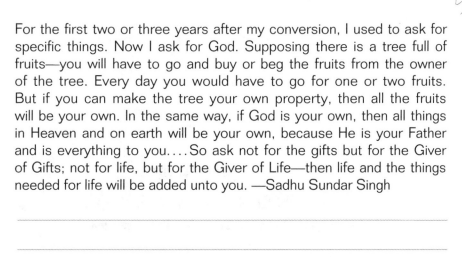

For the first two or three years after my conversion, I used to ask for specific things. Now I ask for God. Supposing there is a tree full of fruits—you will have to go and buy or beg the fruits from the owner of the tree. Every day you would have to go for one or two fruits. But if you can make the tree your own property, then all the fruits will be your own. In the same way, if God is your own, then all things in Heaven and on earth will be your own, because He is your Father and is everything to you....So ask not for the gifts but for the Giver of Gifts; not for life, but for the Giver of Life—then life and the things needed for life will be added unto you. —Sadhu Sundar Singh

DAY THREE

To seek God, we must build into our lives the discipline of solitude and silence. We must respond when the Father calls us to a place of solitude to be alone with Him. *"Therefore I am now going to allure her; I will lead her into the desert and speak tenderly to her"* (Hosea 2:14).

Although prayer is continuous, an ongoing interchange of love between the Father and His child, there must be scheduled time when all of our attention is directed toward God. We must be able to withdraw for a while from the fevered pace of our lives, from the noise and incessant demands, to listen for the still, small voice.

❖

Read the following verse that describes Jesus' discipline of solitude and silence.

Very early in the morning, while it was still dark, Jesus got up, left the house and went off to a solitary place, where he prayed. —Mark 1:35

Why do you think Jesus sought out solitude?

What are the enemies of solitude and silence in your life?

What can you do to overcome these barriers to times of retreating with God?

❖

Week 8, Day 3

PRACTICE A NEW WAY OF PRAYING

Let this thought guide your prayer time today. Journal your prayer.

Father, push back the noise.
Your secrets come wrapped in silence.
—Jennifer Kennedy Dean, *Heart's Cry*

DAY FOUR

Another spiritual discipline to be incorporated into our lives is the discipline of fasting. Andrew Murray, in his book *With Christ in the School of Prayer*, says, "Faith needs a life of prayer in which to grow and keep strong....Prayer needs fasting for its full and perfect development."

What does food do for the body?

What would abstaining from food for a time represent?

Fasting is not a way to influence, impress, or manipulate God. Fasting does not prove anything to God. He knows your heart better than you do (John 2:25; Hebrews 4:13; Psalm 33:15). It is not a hunger strike designed to convince God to release what He has, up to now, held back. Instead, fasting is a way to let go of that which binds us to this physical world—food—in order to receive all our sustenance from the spiritual world.

In fasting, you determine that for a period of time you will deny your physical cravings to focus on your spiritual cravings. You will allow your spiritual hunger to become stronger and more focused. You will feed your spirit with the same enthusiasm with which you feed your body. During a fast, spiritual hunger takes priority over physical hunger. O. Hallesby says, "Fasting loosens the ties which bind us to this world of material things and our surroundings that we may concentrate all our spiritual powers upon the unseen and eternal."

Fasting is not a last-ditch effort to get through to God. Instead, it sharpens our spiritual senses so that God can get through to us. We find the story of a fast in 2 Chronicles 20. Let's examine this incident.

Turn to 2 Chronicles 20.

1. Read verses 1–2. This describes the earth-view. Summarize it—how does the situation look from earth's perspective?

2. Read verses 3–4. Jehoshaphat refused to be fooled by the earth-view. He knew there was more to the situation than meets the eye. He set his sights on what was unseen, rather than what was seen (2 Corinthians 4:18).

What did Jehoshaphat resolve to do?

As a way of inquiring of the Lord, what did Jehoshaphat proclaim?

Why do you think a fast was a vital part of inquiring of the Lord?

3. Read verses 5–12. What do you think Jehoshaphat's purpose was in his spoken prayer?
   a. To use flattery to get God's attention or secure His help.
   b. To remind God of His promises in case He had forgotten.
   c. To convince God that He should help them.
   d. Jehoshaphat was allowing God to bring to mind all the reasons that the people could fully trust Him, and Jehoshaphat was speaking out God's Word. Jehoshaphat was allowing God to build a foothold for their faith.

4. Read verse 12 again. This is the attitude of a fast. Write it out: "We have _____ to face this vast army that is attacking us. We do not know what to do, but _____."

How do you think that helplessness is an asset in prayer?

5. Read verses 14–17. How much did the Lord tell them?
   a. God told them everything He would do and every action He would take. They knew exactly what to expect.
   b. God told them what they were to do to position themselves to receive His victory.

6. Read verses 18–28. When did the people begin to praise God for their victory?

Do you think they had a clear understanding of how God would defeat their enemies as they obeyed His command?

When was the victory finalized? In the spiritual battlefield, or on the material battlefield? (v. 15)

7. Summarize what part fasting played in this event.

❖

Jesus gave clear instructions about fasting. He expected His followers to fast.

"When you fast, do not look somber as the hypocrites do, for they disfigure their faces to show men they are fasting. I tell you the truth, they have received their reward in full. But when you fast, put oil on your head and wash your face, so that it will not be obvious to men that you are fasting, but only to your Father, who is unseen; and your Father, who sees what is done in secret, will reward you." —Matthew 6:16–18

When Jesus said that your Father will reward you, what did He mean? Is He saying that fasting will cause God to give in to requests He has said no to so far? No, He is saying that fasting will sensitize you to the things of the spiritual realm so that you will be more aware of His presence and His present-tense voice. What is God's reward? Himself. *"Surely you have granted him eternal blessings and made him glad with the joy of your presence"* (Psalm 21:6).

Week 8, Day 4

PRACTICE A NEW WAY OF PRAYING

Let this thought guide your prayer time today. Journal your prayer.

Shall not the children of God be faithful in seeking for the treasures hid in heaven, to bring them down in blessing on the world? It is by the unceasing intercession of God's people that His kingdom will come, and His will be done on earth as it is in heaven. —Andrew Murray, *Prayer*

DAY FIVE

To seek God, we must be involved in the discipline of fellowship with believers. We must be an active part of a local church. Christ expresses Himself in His fullness through His body (Ephesians 1:23). Within the context of the body of Christ, we attain our maturity and the full knowledge of God (Ephesians 4:13). The proper working of each individual part causes the growth of the body (Ephesians 4:16).

Watchman Nee uses this illustration to help us understand the fullness of Christ, which is only available through the church: Suppose that you went to the ocean and you filled a container from the ocean. You would have the elements that constitute the ocean in that container. But you would not have the fullness of the ocean in that container. Each individual believer has all of Jesus indwelling him or her. But the fullness of Christ is in the church.

The fullness of God dwells in the Son: *"For God was pleased to have all his fullness dwell in him"* (Colossians 1:19). The fullness of the Son dwells in the church: *"And God placed all things under His feet and appointed him to be head over everything for the church, which is his body, the fullness of him who fills everything in every way"* (Ephesians 1:22–23).

All the resources of heaven are dispensed through the Son: *"For no matter how many promises God has made, they are 'Yes' in Christ"* (2 Corinthians 1:20). All the resources of the Son are dispensed through the church. The church is His body, the vehicle through which He expresses His life.

In learning to hear God's present voice, you don't have to worry about whether you are good at hearing. You can trust that He is good at speaking.

No individual believer will reach full maturity in Christ apart from the body. Ephesians 4:13 is Paul's prayer: *"Until we all reach unity in the faith and in the knowledge of the Son of God and become mature, attaining to the whole measure of the fullness of Christ."* The whole measure of the fullness of Christ is conditioned on reaching *"unity in the faith."* You and I cannot hear God clearly when we are not in unity with the body. Let Paul's prayer be yours: *"May the God who gives endurance and encouragement give you a spirit of unity among yourselves as you follow Christ Jesus"* (Romans 15:5).

Listen to the Father say to you, *"Make every effort to keep the unity of the Spirit through the bond of peace"* (Ephesians 4:3). What attitudes do you need to change or what actions do you need to take to make every effort to keep unity?

Week 8, Day 5

PRACTICE A NEW WAY OF PRAYING

Let this thought guide your prayer time today. Journal your prayer.

The measure of the power of the church today determines the measure of the manifestation of the power of God. For His power is now revealed through the church.... This whole matter can be likened to the flow of water in one's house. Though the water tank of the Water Supply Company is huge, its flow is limited to the diameter of the water pipe in one's own house. If a person wishes to have more flow of water, he will need to enlarge his water pipe. Today the degree of the manifestation of God's power is governed by the capacity of the church.

—Watchman Nee, *The Prayer Ministry of the Church*

Week Eight Anniversary Thought

Recently I bought a new computer desk. Printed on the outside of the box were these words: *Some assembly required.* I opened the box and laid out the pieces. There on the floor of my office was every single component that I would need to put together the desk I now owned. Nothing was missing. Every tool, every screw, every bolt . . . all there.

Along with the pieces were the instructions. Straightforward, clear, and illustrated. Put piece A into piece B and attach them with this particular screw using this tool. When I first started, it seemed pretty overwhelming. It looked like a collection of random, unrelated articles. I couldn't imagine how this pile of stuff on my floor was going to become the desk the package promised.

I decided to do step one. That's all. Just step one. While I was doing step one, I didn't think about step two or step three. Step one went fine, just like the directions said. So I did step two. Step-by-step, doing what was in front of me and not worrying ahead, I saw the desk taking shape. In the end, the desk sitting in my office looked exactly like the desk pictured on the package. Some assembly was required, but everything I needed was already there.

When we are born again into the kingdom of God, I think if we could see from heaven's view, we would see that our new lives are labeled: *Some assembly required.* In fact, that is just what the Scripture says, using different words.

> *His divine power has given us everything we need for life and godliness through our knowledge of him who called us by his own glory and goodness. . . . For this very reason, make every effort to add to your faith goodness; and to goodness, knowledge; and to knowledge, self-control; and to self-control, perseverance; and to perseverance, godliness; and to godliness, brotherly kindness; and to brotherly kindness, love. For if you possess these qualities in*

increasing measure, they will keep you from being ineffective and
unproductive in your knowledge of our Lord Jesus Christ.
—2 Peter 1:3, 5–8

All the pieces are there. The instructions are clear. Don't get overwhelmed by the hugeness of the task, just do the step in front of you. Let the Lord speak this word to you regarding His temple, which you are.

"Be strong and courageous, and do the work. Do not be afraid
or discouraged, for the LORD God, my God, is with you. He will
not fail you or forsake you until all the work for the service of the
temple of the LORD is finished." —1 Chronicles 28:20

Section Three

The Promise of Prayer

The Promise of Prayer

DAY ONE

The promise of prayer is a transformed heart. Through the ongoing discipline of prayer, we are brought into direct and intimate contact with the Father's heart. As we continually behold His glory, we are changed into His image. Our lives begin to reflect Him; our desires begin to reflect His desires. As He has constant access to us, He realigns our vision, recreates our desires, reproduces His heart. Powerful, earth-changing prayer begins in the heart of God and flows through the hearts of His people. The promise of prayer is a heart that matches His.

In your own words, and in terms of your own life, what is the promise that prayer holds?

Once God has taught us and changed us through the prayer process, every promise is ours. Our hearts belong to Him alone and He can plant in them

His divine desires and make them ours. He can release His power and His plans into the world through our prayers. By allowing our lives to be absorbed in His, we can bit by bit be freed of our shortsighted desires to participate in eternity. We can allow the Spirit of God to engage us in what the Father wants to do in the world.

In its simplest analysis prayer—all prayer—has, must have, two parts. First, a God to give....And just as certainly there must be a second factor, a man to receive. Man's willingness is God's channel to the earth...Let it be said that God can do nothing for the man with shut hand and shut life. There must be an open hand and heart and life through which God can give what He longs to. An open life, an open hand, open upward, is the pipeline of communication between the heart of God and this old befooled world. Our prayer is God's opportunity to get into the world that would shut Him out.
—**S. D. Gordon,** *Quiet Talks on Prayer*

The intimacy and trust that grows during the process of prayer is what gives us boldness in prayer. It is the relationship of child to father that makes our words prayer.

Suppose that you ordered a meal at a restaurant. When the server brought your meal, suppose she said, "That looks delicious! I think I'll try a bite." Suppose that she then took a fork and tasted your food. You'd be outraged. You would demand to see the manager. You would insist that the food be taken back.

Suppose, however, that you went to a restaurant with your child. When your meal was served, imagine that your child said, "That looks delicious! I think I'll try a bite." When your child took a bite of your meal, you would not be the least bit upset. This would be a normal exchange between a child and parent.

The difference between the two scenarios is not the words, or even the intent, but the relationship. The parent-child relationship gives boldness and intimacy not available to nonfamily members. The same words take on new meaning in the context of the relationship.

Think of conversations and behaviors that are appropriate in the intimacy of family relationships but are too intimate and bold for less binding relationships. Consider how much freedom and access relationship gives you. As you pray, be aware of how uninhibited and audacious you are allowed to be because you are coming to your Father, not to a distant, unrelated deity.

Relationship changes the way we communicate. Long intimacy, shared history, entwined lives—this kind of relationship colors conversation. For example, I have two sisters. When I am talking to either of them, one of us might say one word or one phrase that sends us into gales of laughter. To an outsider listening in, it would seem that nothing funny had been said. However, because of our long history, a word between us says volumes.

As you live in intimacy with God, you will find the same thing playing out. A mere word may be all the prayer you need to voice in some circumstances. That one word speaks it all. As intimacy grows, the saying of prayer, in many circumstances, becomes simpler.

The kind of intimacy that results in verbal shorthand between you has at its core prolonged, intense interaction. Because of the time invested in intimate communion, an easy and loving familiarity develops. The relationship deepens through focused and deliberate time with Him, then flows naturally through the circumstances of life with an uncontrived delight in each other's company.

Look at the following Scriptures. Write out what each one says to you about your Father-child relationship with God.

Deuteronomy 1:31

Matthew 6:8

Matthew 7:11

Matthew 10:20

Matthew 12:50

Matthew 13:43

Luke 12:30

Luke 12:32

❖

Week 9, Day 1
PRACTICE A NEW WAY OF PRAYING
This is the day the Lord has made; I **will** rejoice and be glad in it.

_____

_____

_____

_____

_____

DAY TWO

In His Word, God makes extravagant promises about prayer. He stands behind His Word. You don't find Him distancing Himself from those lavish promises as some Christians try to do. You don't find Him saying, "I didn't really mean that the way it sounds. I exaggerated to make a point." When prayer doesn't work the way Scripture says it will work, the first thing we do is try to explain away the Scripture.

Do your prayers have power? When you pray, do you consistently see the power of God manifested on the earth? Does your experience in prayer match God's descriptions of prayer's power given in His Word?

"The prayer of a righteous man is powerful and effective," we read in James 5:16. Is that how you would define your prayer life—powerful and effective? Prayer impacts lives and situations on the earth. True prayer works.

Many believers are discouraged about prayer. Secretly, many have reached the conclusion that prayer doesn't work or that prayer only works sometimes. Promises in the Bible regarding prayer seem unreliable, the outcome of prayer unpredictable. As a result, we have watered down or scaled back the Scripture's descriptions of the power of prayer. We expect less from God than He longs to give. After all, how silly we felt having prayed boldly and with great conviction, believing with all our might, only to see our prayers go unanswered. Our faith takes a hit from which it never recovers. Next time, we are more circumspect with our requests. Next time, our expectations are more in line with reality.

Having reached this point, we need to look for ways to explain away the power promised in Scripture. Attempting to justify the lack of powerful praying, we have tried to reduce prayer to an activity that will match our experience, rather than looking for the source of prayer's failure in ourselves.

Do your prayers have power? When you pray, do you consistently see the power of God manifested on the earth?

Suppose you consult a doctor about an ailment and he prescribes a medication. Imagine that the doctor promises that this medication will cure your ailment. "Take this medicine in the prescribed dosage three times a day every day for ten days," he instructs. Suppose that you go home and follow his instructions for a few days. You see little or no improvement, so you begin to doubt the efficacy of the medicine. You take it haphazardly and finally quit taking it altogether. When you return to the doctor for a checkup, you say, "That medicine didn't cure me as you promised it would." Is your accusation accurate? Did the medicine fail? Of course the medicine did not cure your illness. You didn't apply it correctly. You made your own rules. You wanted the medicine to work on your terms. The failing is not in the medicine but in your method of applying the medicine.

This is a picture of how we have come to think of prayer. "Prayer doesn't work like the Bible says it will work," we say. Why not? Could it be because we have tried to make prayer work on our terms and that the failure is not with prayer itself but with our way of praying? Remember that God's Word clearly states that God's power produces results on the earth when a righteous person prays (James 5:16).

Consider the following promises. Underline the extravagant promises.

"Therefore I tell you, whatever you ask for in prayer, believe that you have received it, and it will be yours." —Mark 11:24.

"You may ask me for anything in my name, and I will do it." —John 14:14

"If you remain in me and my words remain in you, ask whatever you wish, and it will be given you." —John 15:7

"In that day you will no longer ask me anything. I tell you the truth, my Father will give you whatever you ask in my name." —John 16:23

"If you believe, you will receive whatever you ask for in prayer." —Matthew 21:22

"'If you can'?" said Jesus. "Everything is possible for him who believes." —Mark 9:23

Week 9, Day 2

PRACTICE A NEW WAY OF PRAYING

This is the day the Lord has made; I **will** rejoice and be glad in it.

_____

_____

_____

_____

_____

DAY THREE

Yesterday you looked at God's astounding promises about prayer. I know that you are astute enough that you noticed that every promise was linked to a relationship requirement. When Jesus said, *"Ask whatever you wish, and it will be given you"* (John 15:7), it was directed toward those who abide in Him and in whom His words abide. The person who is abiding in Christ has desires that are God-shaped. To that person, God gives the keys to the kingdom—prayer and its answer.

Believer, abide in Christ, for there is the school of prayer—mighty, effectual, answer-bringing prayer. Abide in Him and you shall learn what to so many is a mystery: That the secret of the prayer of faith is the life of faith—the life that abides in Christ alone.
—Andrew Murray, *Abide in Christ*

Prayer becomes all that God promises it to be when the pray-er is living a praying life. Out of the life that is abandoned to God and His purposes flows the prayer that God has promised to answer.

There is such a thing as coming into such a sweet relation to the will of God that we are fused into oneness with it. His will becomes ours, and He gladly sets us free to carry our own wishes—they being His first and then ours. —G. Granger Fleming, *The Dynamic of All Prayer*

Yesterday you looked at a series of Scripture promises and you underlined the promise. Go back to those promises now and highlight or circle the relationship requirement.

Make a list of the different relationship requirements linked with prayer promises.

Why do you think that prayer promises are linked to relationship requirements?

❖

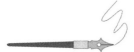

PRACTICE A NEW WAY OF PRAYING

This is the day the Lord has made; I **will** rejoice and be glad in it.

DAY FOUR

The process of purity precedes the promise of power. A pure life is the environment in which power can freely flow.

Refined Like Silver

The Messiah will be like a refiner of silver. In the refining process, heat is applied. The silver and the impurities separate. The pure silver settles to the bottom and the impurities rise to the top where they can be skimmed off. It brings impurities to the surface so they can be removed. *"The crucible for silver and the furnace for gold, but the LORD tests the heart"* (Proverbs 17:3). Do you see? What a crucible does for silver and what a furnace does for gold, God does for the heart.

God chooses the picture of silver to point us to His illustration in creation that teaches us about a pure heart. Silver is a perfect picture of what a pure heart will look like.

Silver is the most malleable of all metals. It can easily be hammered into new shapes. It is moldable.

A pure heart is soft, moldable, and pliable in the hands of the Artist. *"I will give you a new heart and put a new spirit in you; I will remove from you your heart of stone and give you a heart of flesh. And I will put my Spirit in you and move you to follow my decrees and be careful to keep my laws*" (Ezekiel 36:26–27). God will replace our hardened hearts with a soft spirit-heart—a heart that He can shape and mold to match His.

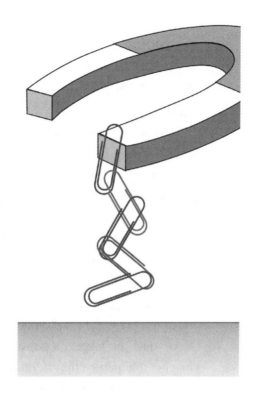

We are clay in the potter's hands. He can take our marred lives and make them into something else, shaping us as seems best to Him (Jeremiah 18:4). Listen to Him saying to you: "*Like clay in the hand of the potter, so are you in my hand*" (Jeremiah 18:6). He wants to mold you into someone beautiful and whole. He wants you to be His artwork. He wants your life to be an expression of His genius. As I respond to Him in obedience, my heart becomes pure silver to be hammered into any shape He desires.

Pure silver is the best conductor of heat and electricity of any element on earth. A conductive substance is a substance through which power moves freely. By means of a conductor, power is transferred from one object to another.

A pure heart—a heart from which all alloys have been removed—is a conductor of God's power into lives and situations on earth. Jesus said, "*If anyone is thirsty, let him come to me and drink. Whoever believes in me, as the Scripture has said, streams of living water will flow from within him*" (John 7:37–38). Do you see? Drink from Him to quench your own thirst, then He will flow from within you in streams of living water. Your life will be the conductor of His Life.

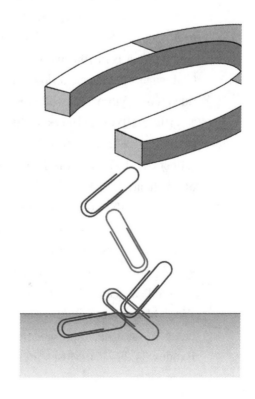

Jesus uses another word that suggests conductive power. He says that He will "draw" people to Himself. He uses a word that suggests an almost irresistible force. God has given us a picture in His creation: magnetism. Think of Jesus in you as a magnet drawing the people in your world to Himself.

What happens when a conductive substance, let's imagine a paper clip, comes within the force field of a magnet? First, the paper clip is drawn to the magnet. Then, when the paper clip has attached to the magnet, the magnetic force begins to flow through it. The paper clip, the conductive substance, becomes a magnet. The magnet's power is flowing through the paper clip. If a second paper clip comes into contact with the first, it, too, will become a magnet because the magnetic force will flow from the first paper clip into the second.

What happens if the first paper clip loses contact with the magnet? It loses its magnetism! It did not have power of its own; it only had the ability to conduct the magnet's power. It had induced magnetism. Apart from the magnet, the paper clip can do nothing. Separated from the power, the conductor is useless, like dead branches separated from the vine.

God does not give you power. He exercises His power through you. He has created you of a Spirit-substance that is conductive. His power can flow through you.

God does not give you power. He exercises His power through you.

Where is the epicenter of God's power on the earth? You know what the epicenter is. It's the place on the surface of the earth where the earthquake occurs. Everything else is the result of waves of power radiating out from the epicenter. Where is the epicenter of God's power on the earth? *"Now to him who is able to do immeasurably more than all we ask or imagine, according to **his power** that is at work **within us**"* (Ephesians 3:20). The epicenter of God's power is in you and in me. We are the conductors of the power of God. God wants His power to flow through you in undiluted strength. He wants to rid you of anything that will hinder the flow.

Pure silver reflects light better than any other element. Purified silver reflects without distortion. The desires of a pure heart exactly reflect the desires of the Father. A pure heart is an undistorted reflection of His heart.

What is the process by which we come to reflect Him? *"And we, who with unveiled faces all reflect the Lord's glory, are being transformed into his likeness with ever-increasing glory, which comes from the Lord, who is the Spirit"* (2 Corinthians 3:18).

Paul, in using the phrase "with unveiled face," is referring to Moses. When Moses met with the Lord, the skin on his face shone so brightly from being in the Lord's presence that Moses had to veil his countenance (see Exodus 34:29–35). Moses literally reflected God's glory. Paul is telling us that because we are in the Lord's presence, we, too, reflect His glory just as a mirror reflects an image. How does a mirror reflect? It absorbs light bouncing off an object and projects it back in exactly the same configuration. It absorbs and reflects.

As we absorb Him by being continually in His presence, we reflect Him. As we absorb Him, we are being changed into an exact reflection of Him. We are being transformed—changed from the inside out; structurally changed. We are being changed into His likeness progressively, *"with ever-increasing glory."* How is this changing being accomplished? *"Which comes from the Lord, who is the Spirit."* The Spirit is doing the changing as we continue in His presence.

A pure heart is a heart that reflects His desires. When my heart is pure, His desires are poured into my heart so that they become my desires and are expressed through my prayers. Impurity will distort the reflection, will cause it not to be exact. This is why the Father wants to make you pure. He wants you to desire your highest good. He wants to give you the desires of your heart.

Silver is resistant to corrosion from the atmosphere. Atmospheric corrosives cannot destroy silver, but can only produce surface tarnish.

A pure heart is resistant to corrosion and corruption by outside influences. *"Do not conform any longer to the pattern of this world, but be transformed by the renewing of your mind. Then you will be able to test and approve what God's will is—his good, pleasing and perfect will"* (Romans 12:2).

Paul contrasts two ways of changing: conforming and being transformed. The word "conform" means to be changed from the outside or to be squeezed into a mold. The word "transform" means to be changed from within. Both words mean to change forms, but one indicates change from the outside and one from the inside. Paul warns that the world wants to force you into a form that is not a natural fit. God wants to change your outward form so that it fits your inner being. He wants your inward self to be authentically reflected in your personality and lifestyle. His will for you is a perfect fit. The world's pattern is restrictive, diminishing, smothering. His will for you is beneficial and pleasing.

God wants to make you resistant to the forces and elements that would corrode your beauty by trying to conform you to a pattern that does not fit you. He wants you to be forged into His image so that the corrosion in the world will not penetrate your life and diminish you. He will bring this about by renewing your mind—making your mind something different than it was before. Under His influence, you will begin to know, understand, and embrace God's good, pleasing, and perfect will.

Power flows from purity. Seek purity and you will find power.

List the four qualities of silver that describe the heart of a power pray-er and write out your thoughts about what God is saying directly to you about each of these qualities.

1.

2.

3.

4.

Week 9, Day 4

PRACTICE A NEW WAY OF PRAYING

This is the day the Lord has made; I **will** rejoice and be glad in it.

_____ ## DAY FIVE

God is at work in you continually creating a life that is available for all that He longs to put into it. The promise underlying all prayer is that God has pledged Himself—bound Himself in blood-sealed covenant—to accomplish *in you* what He requires *of you*. "I **will** give them a heart to know Me. I **will** put My laws in their minds and on their hearts. I **will** move them to follow My ways. I **will** put a new spirit in them."

Why has He put into place a process of prayer? Because He is changing you from one degree of glory to the next. He is fashioning a heart like His. He is preparing your life to receive His answers. He is making you the dwelling place of His Spirit—the place where His glory is manifested.

Dear Friend, put away childish things—little, flesh-shaped desires; short-sighted, earth-bound understanding. Yield yourself to His bigger agenda. Let Him do more than you can ask or even think. Let Him do His full and mighty work in you. Then every prayer promise is yours.

> The Spirit's quiet whisper
> Bids me bow before Your throne
> 'Til my heart's deepest yearnings
> Are the echo of Your own.

What has been the goal of your prayer life? Has it been to get God to perform for you? How has your goal begun to change?

Week 9, Day 5

PRACTICE A NEW WAY OF PRAYING

This is the day the Lord has made; I **will** rejoice and be glad in it.

Week Nine Anniversary Thought

I learned a new word recently. It's a French word, *terroir*. It refers to all the natural conditions that come together to influence the composition of a grape and consequently a wine. It describes the cumulative effect of the climate, soil, and landscape upon the character of a wine. Different terroirs produce different qualities in a wine even when the same grape is grown. So, even when one has the perfect grape and performs all the requisite tasks for its growth, if the terroir is inferior, so will be the wine.

The Lord wants to make your life like a watered garden. He wants your life to be lush with the Spirit's fruit. He wants His life to be on display in you. That's why He works on the terroir of your life. He makes sure your roots go deep. He makes sure the soil of your heart is tilled and fertilized. He makes sure that you have the right seasons at the right time. He describes you like this:

> *"He will be like a tree planted by the water*
> *that sends out its roots by the stream.*
> *It does not fear when heat comes;*
> *its leaves are always green.*
> *It has no worries in a year of drought*
> *and never fails to bear fruit."*
> —Jeremiah 17:8

All because the Lord, the Vineyard Owner, gives careful attention to the terroir of your life.

Faith Is Required

PRACTICE A NEW WAY OF PRAYING

This week, hear the Father speaking to you about the kingdom and respond to His voice. Use the daily meditations provided.

DAY ONE

"Have faith in God," Jesus answered. "I tell you the truth, if anyone says to this mountain, 'Go, throw yourself into the sea,' and does not doubt in his heart but believes that what he says will happen, it will be done for him. Therefore I tell you, whatever you ask for in prayer, believe that you have received it, and it will be yours." —Mark 11:22–24

Faith and prayer are inseparable. Faith fuels prayer. Prayer expresses faith. The two are intertwined. One does not exist without the other. But what is faith?

Is faith a feeling that can be worked up? Is faith feeling sure that we know what God will do? Does faith have anything to do with feeling? It is very important that we look closely at faith because a misguided understanding of faith and how it operates has caused many pray-ers to lose heart.

In Lewis Carroll's *Through the Looking Glass*, Alice has this conversation with the White Queen:

"Now I'll give you something to believe. I'm just one hundred and one, five months and a day."

"I can't believe that!" said Alice.

"Can't you?" the Queen said in a pitying tone. "Try again: draw a long breath, and shut your eyes."

Alice laughed. "There's no use trying," she said; "One can't believe impossible things."

"I daresay you haven't had much practice," said the Queen. "When I was your age, I always did it for half-an-hour a day. Why, sometimes I've believed as many as six impossible things before breakfast."

This, of course, is a silly conversation in a make-believe story. But it is not far from the way we sometimes are taught to stir up faith. "If you can just believe hard enough, you can make God do anything," the thinking goes. It's up to you—you must believe. You can believe God into things if you try hard enough.

Faith is not "believing real hard." Faith is not shutting your eyes and drawing a long breath and willing yourself to believe something. You can make yourself believe anything, true or not. Believing it won't make God do it. Belief is one thing; faith is something else.

Because many believers have mistaken belief for faith, they have had experiences in prayer that are discouraging and disappointing. They have believed with all their might that God would perform in a certain way that seemed best to the pray-er. I repeat, you can make yourself believe anything. Perhaps the pray-er has wrapped verses of Scripture around his belief; perhaps he has listed all the ways that God will be glorified by performing as the pray-er believes He will perform; perhaps he has spoken his belief to others, putting himself on the line for it. All this the pray-er has done with the best intentions, mistakenly thinking he is exercising faith. But it is not faith, it is belief. In this approach, there is an underlying, unconscious thought that a pray-er can "believe God into something," that by putting His reputation on the line, God will be forced to come through. Many people who are using this method refer to the promise in Psalm 31:17: "*Let me not be put to shame, O LORD, for I have cried out to you.*"

No matter what you do, you will never be able to manipulate God. Your prayers will never do anything except release God's power for God's purposes.

Friends, it won't work. No matter what you do, you will never be able to manipulate God. Your prayers will never do anything except release God's power for God's purposes. On the other hand, your prayers will always release God's power for God's purposes. Faith is not knowing *how* God will bring His will into being; faith is knowing *that* God will bring His will into being.

Faith has only one focus: God. "*Have faith in God*" (Mark 11:22). When your faith is in God, not in your own idea of what God should do and how He should do it, then faith has substance. The person who is living a praying life is living a life of faith. That person understands that prayer is always releasing the power of God for the purposes of God. Therefore, whatever direction a situation takes once prayer has begun, it is taking the direction that will accomplish the purposes of God. That's faith.

❖

How do you resolve the following hypothetical situations?

Two families, both Christian families who believe in prayer, learn that a child is fatally ill. Both pray for healing. Both pray with equal fervency, with equal faith, with equal frequency. One child dies, the other is miraculously healed.

Two Christians lose their jobs unexpectedly. Both turn to the Lord, determining to look to Him for all guidance and all supply. Both pray and both do all they can to find new employment. One gets a new and better job immediately. The other spends many months unemployed and is finally employed at a job not even equal with the job he lost.

A Christian feels strongly led to take an active role in praying for a political election. He feels sure that Candidate A exhibits the values and character traits of a godly leader and prays for Candidate A's victory. Candidate B wins.

In response to the prayer of faith, God begins to release His power to accomplish His purposes in each situation. His purpose in each situation is worked out differently. He does not have "one-size-fits-all" answers. God's agenda is always bigger than the immediate circumstances. The immediate circumstances are going to merge with an eternal agenda. Faith says: "I believe in God—in His love, in His power, in His wisdom. I know that He is in the process of bringing His best plan. God will not allow any difficulty to have mastery over me. He is using the circumstance to do something He couldn't do without it."

You do not have to be able to predict how God will act in order to have faith. I can hear some of you now. I know what you're thinking. "That can't be right. I have to believe. If I don't believe, if I doubt, I can't expect anything from the Lord." To your mind will come such Scriptures as this one:

But when he asks, he must believe and not doubt, because he who doubts is like a wave of the sea, blown and tossed by the wind. That man should not think he will receive anything from the Lord; he is a double-minded man, unstable in all he does. —James 1:6–8

Or maybe you're thinking about Matthew 13:58: "*And he did not do many miracles there because of their lack of faith.*"

Let's talk about these. Let's look at the passage in James first. A misunderstanding of this passage causes much discouragement and condemnation. First, keep these sentences in their context. James is talking about asking for wisdom. "*If any of you lacks wisdom, he should ask God, who gives generously to all without finding fault, and it will be given to him*" (James 1:5). Wisdom in any given situation is yours for the asking. When God gives you wisdom, James says, don't begin to doubt it and second-guess it. If you do, you will waver back and forth in your thinking and in your emotions. You will not receive what God has available for you because it is your obedience to the wisdom He gives you that opens the door for His provision.

So James is not saying that every time you pray you must believe that God is going to do what you think He should do. He is talking about one kind of praying—prayer for wisdom. He is saying to keep a steady course based on what God is leading you to do.

Now let's look at Jesus' experience in Matthew 13. The account starts in verse 53.

When Jesus had finished these parables, he moved on from there. Coming to his hometown, he began teaching the people in their synagogue, and they were amazed. "Where did this man get this wisdom and these miraculous powers?" they asked. "Isn't this the carpenter's son? Isn't his mother's name Mary, and aren't his brothers James, Joseph, Simon and Judas? Aren't all his sisters with us? Where then did this man get all these things?" And they took offense at him. But Jesus said to them, "Only in his hometown and in his own house is a prophet without honor." And he did not do many miracles there because of their lack of faith.

You will notice that the people did not disbelieve that He could do miracles. In fact, they were amazed at His miraculous powers. It was not doubt about what He could do that is called "their lack of faith." It was their refusal to embrace who He was. They had confidence in His ability to do miracles—they had belief. But they did not have faith. They were not willing to abandon themselves to Him, trusting Him to be all they needed or desired.

We will continue to look at the difference between belief and faith this week. But you can begin to see the difference between believing in an outcome and having faith in God.

Week 10, Day 1 • Prayer Journal

PRACTICE A NEW WAY OF PRAYING

Frequently we hold on so tightly to the good that we do know that we cannot receive the greater good that we do not know. God has to help us let go of our tiny vision in order to release the greater good he has in store for us....A settled peace is the most frequent experience of those who have trod the path of relinquishment.
—Richard Foster, *Prayer*

_____

_____

_____

DAY TWO

Let's go back to the central question: What is faith? Faith is not a feeling. Faith is not "feeling sure." You can be exercising faith and at the same time be filled with feelings of uncertainty. As you mature in your faith-walk, as you gain more confidence in how to operate in faith, your feelings will begin to match your faith; but your feelings are not the measure of your faith.

The prayer of faith comes from the life of faith. Faith is a way of living. Faith is born into you when you are born into the Kingdom of God, and it is the spiritual organ that enables you to function in the spiritual realm. Are you using it or is it lying dormant?

Let me illustrate what I mean with this parable. You and I, earth persons, have organs that suit us to planet Earth's environment. Planet Mars has a different ecosystem. Its air has a different makeup than earth's air. Our earth lungs are not designed to work in the air of Mars. Therefore, we don't go to Mars.

Imagine, though, that you and I had an organ we knew nothing about because our bodies had never needed its function. It has been dormant in us and we had no knowledge of its existence. This organ, we discover, would be activated if we stepped into the environment of Mars. It is the organ that would permit us to operate and function on Mars. All this time we were kept from Mars because we didn't know that we had the organ that would make us functional in Mars's ecosystem! We would have limited ourselves unnecessarily.

Faith is a spiritual organ that makes it possible for you to function in the spiritual realm and to live out spiritual reality. However, until you step out into that realm, it lies dormant. Faith is given to you at your new birth, but lies dormant until you begin to put it to use. Once you begin to put it to use, all the riches of the spiritual realm are at your disposal. *"For all things belong to you, whether Paul or Apollos or Cephas or the world or life or death or things present or things to come; all things belong to you, and you belong to Christ; and Christ belongs to God"* (1 Corinthians 3:21–23 NASB).

A spiritual kingdom lies all about us, enclosing us, embracing us, altogether within reach of our inner selves, waiting for us to recognize it. God Himself is waiting our response to His presence. The eternal world will come alive to us the moment we reckon upon its reality.

O God, Quicken to life every power within me, that I may lay hold on eternal things. Open my eyes that I may see; give me acute spiritual perception; enable me to taste Thee and know that Thou art good. Make heaven more real to me than any earthly thing has ever been.

—A. W. Tozer, *The Pursuit of God*

Underline the words or phrases that answer the question: How does the Scripture tell us that we obtained faith?

"It is Jesus' name and the faith that comes through him that has given this complete healing to him, as you can all see." —Acts 3:16

For by the grace given me I say to every one of you: Do not think of yourself more highly than you ought, but rather think of yourself with sober judgment, in accordance with the measure of faith God has given you. —Romans 12:3

For it is by grace you have been saved, through faith—and this not from yourselves, it is the gift of God. —Ephesians 2:8

Not only do you have a spiritual organ called faith, but you also have a set of spiritual senses that enable you to operate effectively in the spiritual realm. When you were born into the physical world, you were born with a set of physical senses. By means of these senses you interpret, understand, and interact with your physical world. Through your senses you receive knowledge about your physical world and that knowledge forms the basis of your behavior. For example, when your sense of hearing tells you that a car is speeding at you from behind, you jump out of the way. If your sense of sight tells you the plant in your office needs to be watered, you water it. If your sense of smell tells you the milk in your refrigerator has soured, you dispose of it. You base your actions on the knowledge transmitted to you by your senses. You accept what your senses tell you (belief) and you act on it (faith).

You have learned that your physical senses are reliable. "Seeing is believing," the saying goes. "I would never have believed it, except I heard it with my own ears," you might have said.

Suppose that I'm standing in a room full of people. How would I know that the room was full of people? My senses would tell me so. I would see them, hear them, touch them. Through my senses, I would have certain, sure knowledge that the room was full of people. Now suppose that someone says to me, "There's no one here. This room is empty." Would I believe that person? Of course not, because I have learned by experience that my senses are reliable and accurate transmitters of information about my world. I would have unwavering faith that the room was full of people because my senses told me so. I would know.

When you were born into the kingdom of God, you were born with a set of spiritual senses.

Look up these Scriptures and list the spiritual senses they describe.

Psalm 34:8

Psalm 119:103

Ephesians 1:18

Isaiah 50:5

Matthew 11:15

Your spiritual senses are the means by which you know, understand, and respond to your spiritual world. Faith grows as a result of responding to your spiritual senses. *"Faith comes from hearing the message, and the message is heard through the word of Christ"* (Romans 10:17). Faith comes from hearing the message. Does that mean everyone whose physical ears hear the message receives faith? The whole context of the message in Romans 10 is that not everyone who hears the message with physical ears accepts it. Only in those who hear the message "through the word of Christ" is faith produced. "Word" in this verse is *rhema*—the present voicing of a word; the speaking word. The one who hears with spiritual ears—who hears Christ Himself speaking the message into his heart—finds that the message gives birth to faith. The Living Voice stimulates the faith-organ and causes it to function properly.

Faith is your God-given capacity to receive and act on spiritual knowledge. *"By faith Abraham...obeyed"* (Hebrews 11:8).

Faith Is Born of Firsthand Experience with God
When Scripture tells us how to know God, it uses "sense" words.

Taste and see that the LORD is good. —Psalm 34:8

How sweet are your words to my taste, sweeter than honey to my mouth!
—Psalm 119:103

I pray also that the eyes of your heart may be enlightened in order that you may know. —Ephesians 1:18

The Sovereign LORD has opened my ears. —Isaiah 50:5

For we are to God the aroma of Christ. —2 Corinthians 2:15

Why do you suppose God uses these sense words to tell us how to know Him? Consider this: How would you describe the taste of a fresh strawberry to someone who has never tasted a fresh strawberry? You couldn't. A strawberry tastes like a strawberry. Things that we know through our senses, we have to learn firsthand. You could not describe the smell of the ocean to someone who has never smelled the ocean. You can't describe the sound of a thunderstorm to someone who has never heard a thunderstorm.

So it is with knowing God. You can only know Him by firsthand experience. Knowing God produces faith. You cannot trust the promises. You must trust the Promiser. A promise is only as reliable as the person who makes it. If you don't know the promiser, you have no way of knowing whether or not to rely on the promise. "*Let us hold unswervingly to the hope we profess, for **he who promised is faithful**" (Hebrews 10:23). In order to live by faith, we have to be *"fully persuaded that God [has] power to do what he [has] promised"* (Romans 4:21).

Faith can only come through a direct, firsthand encounter with Jesus. Belief can come through secondhand information, but belief is not faith. I can believe things without putting my faith in them. For example, I can believe that a chair will hold me up. However, if I never sit in the chair—if I never put my faith in it—I will never move from belief to certain knowledge. "*Faith is being sure of what we hope for and certain of what we do not see*" (Hebrews 11:1). Why does it matter whether I have belief or faith?

Let's say that I believe that a certain chair will hold me up, but I have never sat in that chair. I am in the "belief" position. Now my adversary can say, "That chair will never hold you up."

"Of course it will. I believe it will," I reply.

"How do you know?" my adversary taunts.

"Because I can see that it is constructed of sturdy materials. I can see where the center of gravity would be. I'm sure the chair would hold me up."

Then my adversary could say, "But there may be a hidden flaw you don't know about."

My only answer could be, "You're right. There could be."

Belief can be shaken. Faith cannot.

Suppose that I take the faith position and sit in the chair. Now my adversary can say, "That chair will never hold you up." To which I will reply, "Of course it will."

My adversary will then say, "How do you know?" And I will reply, "Because it is." I will overcome his attack with the word of my testimony (Revelation 12:11). Faith cannot be shaken. Faith comes from firsthand experience.

Suppose that I came to earth from another planet with the assignment of learning all I can about the earth. Suppose that I wanted to learn about earth rocks. Someone tells me, "Earth rocks are hard." That becomes what I believe. With all my heart, I believe that earth rocks are hard. However, no matter how much emotion I invest in my belief, it is only belief. It came to me secondhand and secondhand information can only produce belief.

Suppose that someone else told me later that earth rocks are soft and spongy. Now what would I believe? I'd sometimes lean toward believing that rocks were hard, and other times I'd be convinced that they were soft. I'd be like a wave of the sea, blown and tossed by the wind. I'd waver between two opinions.

Get to know the Promiser for yourself, and it will be easy to trust His promises.

What would be the only remedy for my dilemma? I would have to touch an earth rock for myself. Then I would know—not just believe—that earth rocks are hard. Never again would I wonder if they're really soft. I would have faith that earth rocks are hard. Faith cannot be shaken.

If you find yourself shifting back and forth between confidence and anxiety, if you find that your mind and emotions can never fully be at rest, probably you have strong belief, but have not moved on to faith. You cannot get faith from any source except God Himself. Get to know the Promiser for yourself, and it will be easy to trust His promises. Give Him every opportunity to prove Himself strong in your behalf. Let Him take responsibility for moving you on to faith. Rest in Him.

Look at a situation facing you right now. What is your earth-bound assessment telling you about it? What do your spiritual senses tell you about it?

PRACTICE A NEW WAY OF PRAYING

Heir to My riches, understand this Kingdom principle: Because you are fully instated as a citizen of My Kingdom, you never have to worry about anything. All the energy that citizens of the world-kingdom expend scurrying after earth-supplies, you will put to eternal use. Everything you need to operate in the earth environment, I have already set aside and earmarked for you. It is yours. Turn your energy and your passion to seeking and possessing kingdom riches.

—Jennifer Kennedy Dean, *Secret Place of the Most High*

DAY THREE

You do not have to find more faith or work up more faith. Faith will increase as your spiritual senses mature. When a baby is born into the physical world, that baby has the sense of sight but cannot distinguish and identify shapes. The baby has the sense of hearing, but cannot divide sounds into words and ascribe meaning to them The baby's senses have to mature over time and with practice. It is the same with your spiritual senses. Knowing how to hear God clearly and reliably is learned by the slow discipline of prayer and obedience. God will guide you gently and steadily. He will enlighten the eyes of your heart. He will teach you how to keep in step with the Spirit.

I often am asked this question: Does faith create the reality? In other words, did faith make something happen? My answer is, "Faith did not create the reality. Faith made it possible for you to experience the reality." Remember yesterday when you read the illustration of sitting in a chair as moving from belief to faith? Well, suppose that I believed the chair would hold me up so I sat in the chair. Suppose that what I believed about the chair had not been true—it wasn't really solid enough to hold me up. When I sat in the chair, the chair would have collapsed no matter how much I believed it wouldn't. If, on the other hand, what I believed was true—the chair did hold me up—did it hold me up because I believed it would? Do you see? My sitting in the chair (faith) caused me to experience the reality in my own life that the chair would support me.

Faith is not just how you deal with certain promises, but a continual interaction with the spiritual realm. Remember that faith is a spiritual organ through which you receive and use spiritual resources. In the earth realm, for example, your eyes are the organ through which you receive light. Light is pressing in around you, but your eyes have to be open to receive it. Your lungs are the organ through which you receive oxygen. Oxygen is pressing in around you, but your lungs have to function in order to take it in. The Spirit-resources of heaven are available and pressing in around you, but you must live by faith in order to receive and use them.

You already have access to the eternal resources of God, the spiritual aspects of reality. Faith is how you take them into your life and use them. God's promises are not for someday, they're for today.

For he has rescued us from the dominion of darkness and brought us into the kingdom of the Son he loves. —Colossians 1:13

Praise be to the God and Father of our Lord Jesus Christ, who has blessed us in the heavenly realms with every spiritual blessing in Christ. —Ephesians 1:3

And God raised us up with Christ and seated us with him in the heavenly realms in Christ Jesus. —Ephesians 2:6

For you died, and your life is now hidden with Christ in God. —Colossians 3:3

When God's Word speaks of the spiritual world, of the resources of Christ, the action is spoken of as already completed. Faith brings the available resources of God into our lives.

When we are operating in faith, we are accessing the resources of heaven for the circumstances of earth. To live by faith is to operate in the spiritual realm with confidence, the same way you operate in your physical world with confidence. Your physical senses give you the information you need in order to function well in your physical environment. Your spiritual senses give you the information you need in order to function productively in the spiritual realm.

Before you knew Jesus personally, you were a citizen of the kingdom of the world (also called the kingdom of darkness.) When you allowed the Spirit to take up residence in you—when you accepted Jesus' lordship over your life—the Scripture says that you changed your citizenship. You became a citizen of the kingdom of heaven. "*For he has rescued us from the dominion of darkness and brought us into the kingdom of the Son he loves*" (Colossians 1:13). When you belonged to the world's kingdom, you were a foreigner to the spiritual kingdom. The kingdom of God was not accessible to you. You had no rights in it and no inheritance there. Now, though, everything has changed. Now the kingdom belongs to you.

Because you've moved into a new land, with new landmarks and new language and new customs, you have to learn the culture of spirit. Even though you now belong to the eternal kingdom, you may still feel more at home in the world kingdom. You are accustomed to the world's ways of operating; you understand the nuances of the language. But you feel insecure and out-of-place in your new home. You are not as confident about how to live and move and interpret the spiritual kingdom. It's as if you have a whole new language—in fact, a whole new culture—to learn. And so, the temptation is to keep a foot in both places. When you do that, the world-kingdom will slow your progress in the spiritual realm. The familiar ways of the world continue to pull you back.

When a person is going to learn a new language, experts say it is best to simply move into the culture and begin to absorb it. That's what you'll have to do to become proficient in the spiritual realm. Move in—lock, stock, and barrel. At first, you will feel out of place. You will not understand some of the ways of the new kingdom. The language of the spiritual realm will seem foreign to you. But with time, you will absorb the new ways. If you won't go back, you will become more familiar with and comfortable in operating in the life of faith than you are in the life of flesh. Flesh-thinking will seem foreign to you.

What situation are you dealing with in which you know you need to operate in the ways of the Spirit rather than in the ways of flesh?

Ask God to use this situation to train you further in the rights and privileges of your kingdom citizenship.

Week 10, Day 3

PRACTICE A NEW WAY OF PRAYING

Citizen of My Kingdom, I have already transferred your citizenship from the world-kingdom to My Kingdom. The world-kingdom is limited to the boundaries of time and space and senses; My Kingdom has no limits—no boundaries imposed by geography, no restraints dictated by time, no finite apprehension of truth narrowly defined by sense-knowledge. You are now a citizen and inhabitant of the Kingdom of power and eternity. The riches of My Kingdom are at your disposal. Seek the Kingdom—study the landscape, learn the governing principles, become acquainted with the natural resources—so that you can make full use of your citizenship.
—Jennifer Kennedy Dean, *Secret Place of the Most High*

_____

_____

_____

_____

DAY FOUR

The Book of 2 Kings records an instance in the life of Elisha that illustrates the difference between using physical senses and using spiritual senses. The king of Syria was angry because Elisha had warned the king of Israel about his plans several time. He decided to ambush Elisha.

Then he sent horses and chariots and a strong force there. They went by night and surrounded the city. When the servant of the man of God got up and went out early the next morning, an army with horses and chariots had surrounded the city. "Oh, my lord, what shall we do?" the servant asked. "Don't be afraid," the prophet answered. "Those who are with us are more than those who are with them." —2 Kings 6:14–16

Elisha's servant, judging by that which his physical senses perceived, was undoubtedly confused. He and Elisha were looking at the same scene and seeing two different situations. As far as he could see, it was him and Elisha against a great army of Syrians. Then came the turning point.

And Elisha prayed, "O LORD, open his eyes so he may see." Then the LORD opened the servant's eyes, and he looked and saw the hills full of horses and chariots of fire all around Elisha. —2 Kings 6:17

God allowed the servant to see with his physical eyes what Elisha saw with his spiritual eyes. The facts of the situation did not change. Only his understanding of the facts changed. Once his spiritual eyes were opened, he was able to perceive and experience what had always been true.

When Elisha said, "Those who are with us are more than those who are with them," the word "more" means both more in number and more in might—more quantitatively and more qualitatively. I believe that John was echoing this sentence when he wrote, *"The one who is in you is greater than the one who is in the world"* (1 John 4:4). When your spiritual senses perceive the full truth of the situation, your faith organ is activated. Ask the Lord to open your eyes so that you may see.

Why do you need to be able to perceive the truth in the spiritual realm in order to pray in faith? Why has God given you *"the Spirit who is from God, that we may understand what God has freely given us*" (1 Corinthians 2:12)? He wants you to know what is freely available to you so that you can access it. When you know that God has everything prepared for you, you do not have to pray with fear or uncertainty. You can pray with faith.

Faith, as with everything in the spiritual realm, is initiated by God. Jesus is the author of our faith. Faith begins with God, who speaks His promises, thereby awakening faith. If God had not promised us anything, we would not expect anything from Him. He authors faith, just as He authors prayer. He did not stir up faith in order to disappoint you. When faith rises up in you, kind of like a jolt of adrenaline to your spirit, God has caused it to be so. He is causing you to hold out your faith-hand so that He can place His blessings in it.

Faith in its active form is called "obedience." Faith in its spoken form is called "prayer." Faith opens the way for God to display His power on the earth in every situation.

Write out the definition of faith found in Hebrews 11:1.

Now, rewrite it in your own words, applying it directly to specific needs and circumstances in your life.

Week 10, Day 4

PRACTICE A NEW WAY OF PRAYING

Child, I know all about the situation that is worrying you right now. I knew about it before you did. Believe me when I tell you it is finished. Your prayers are bringing the finished work out of the spiritual realm to establish it in the material realm. You do not see the finished work in the earth environment yet, but earth is not your home. Do you know why you are having difficulty believing right now? Because you have only looked at the situation in the artificial light of the earth-kingdom. Earth-kingdom's light only shows up the need. Bring it to Me. Spend time with Me in your true Kingdom. Look at it in the Eternal Light. I will blot out the need and illumine only the supply. Come!
—Jennifer Kennedy Dean, *Secret Place of the Most High*

DAY FIVE

The beginning point of every prayer of faith is the prayer of relinquishment. Before we can begin to hear God tell us what and how to pray in any given matter, we must let the Father bring us to the point that "Not my will, but Thine be done" is our true, heartfelt, authentic prayer. This is not a prayer of resignation to the circumstances; it's not throwing in the towel and giving up. The prayer of relinquishment can only come from a heart that knows the heart of the Father-Shepherd. We can abandon ourselves fully to His will because we know that His heart does not contain one thought or desire toward us that is anything less than the highest possible good.

The prayer of relinquishment is the highest expression of full and mature faith in the Father. It is the truest experience of dying to your flesh in order to live by the Spirit. It is handing over control to the One who is worthy of such trust. The prayer of relinquishment is a statement of absolute surrender. This has become my prayer of relinquishment. "*Father, glorify your name*" (John 12:28). Whatever it takes, Father; whatever path it sets me on, Father; whatever dying to self I have to do, Father. Glorify Your name!"

Write out a list of situations you are praying about. After each, write: "Father, glorify Your name" and today's date. Take the time with the Father to fully relinquish everything on your list.

Once your flesh is out of the way with its self-centered demands and time-bound outlook, the power of God can begin to flow freely. He can begin to speak to you about what and how to pray. He can give you specific instructions about any actions you should take.

Catherine Marshall's book *Something More* tells her own journey about learning how to pray for healing. In it, she tells about learning to pray the prayer of relinquishment. She recounts a story of the healing of a woman named Maude Blanford. One of the turning points of this story is Mrs. Blanford's relinquishment to whatever God wanted to do about her illness. She found afterward that the Lord began to give her very clear instructions.

It's an interesting story, and I suggest that you read it. But I want to quote a couple of paragraphs that I think will help us see what the prayer of relinquishment releases.

About this point she commented to me, "I learned a lot about the difference between self-effort, which is the result of our human will to live and the self-effort that's obedience to what God tells us to do. We have to cooperate with what we see God doing, as Jesus puts it."

She was so right. After our relinquishment, when the initiative passes to God, we need to follow willingly, obediently, trustingly. There must be no running out ahead of Him, but also no lying back limp or passive either. Instead we learn to listen and we follow.

We can only exercise faith if we can hear God. Faith is responding to the present-tense voice of the Father. Faith is not believing *something*. Faith is believing *Someone*. Faith is not committing yourself to an idea, but to a Person.

Hebrews 11 is a chapter about faith. The first 3 verses define faith; the rest of the verses describe faith as it is expressed. The writer of Hebrews says, "*This [faith] is what the ancients were commended for*" (v. 2).

Faith is not believing something. Faith is believing Someone. Faith is not committing yourself to an idea, but to a Person.

Turn to Hebrews 11 and think through what God is saying. Read verses 1–3.

Focus on verse 3. Let me quote it from the New American Standard Version and then from *The Message* by Eugene Peterson.

By faith we understand that the worlds were prepared by the word of God, so that what is seen was not made out of things which are visible.
—Hebrews 11:3 (NASB)

By faith, we see the world called into existence by God's word, what we see created by what we don't see. —Hebrews 11:3 (*The Message*)

1. What called the world into existence?

2. Is God's Word, which created the world, visible or invisible?

3. Is the world visible or invisible?

4. If the world was created by God's Word, then the visible was created from the invisible. What we see is made out of what we don't see.

❖

This sentence (v. 3) is the thesis statement for this whole treatise on faith. From this statement, the writer begins to document his case. Faith, he is saying, is when the invisible power of God's Word—that is, His *rhema*, His present-tense word—produces a visible effect on the earth.

Now read through verses 4–40. How does the Scripture define faith?

1. *"By faith Abel offered"* (v. 4).
2. *"By faith Noah...built"* (v. 7).
3. *"By faith Abraham...obeyed and went"* (v. 8).
4. *"By faith Abraham...offered Isaac"* (v. 17).
5. *"By faith Isaac blessed"* (v. 20).

On and on it goes. These people who are held up as examples of faith were commended for what they did—not felt—in response to God's voice. What defined the action as "faith"? It was an action taken because God said to take it!

When God spoke and a human acted on what He said, His power became visible on the earth. The invisible became visible through the faith responses of humans.

In Hebrews 11:6 we are told that *"without faith it is impossible to please God."* Romans 14:23 says that *"everything that does not come from faith is sin."* What is the starting point for faith? God's voice. So anything that is done from any other motivation is sin; it does not please God. God does not find pleasure in His people doing "good" things and obeying the rules. He finds pleasure in His people *obeying His voice.* Look at this incident from the life of King Saul.

"But I did obey the LORD," Saul said. "I went on the mission the LORD assigned me. I completely destroyed the Amalekites and brought back Agag their king. The soldiers took sheep and cattle from the plunder, the best of what was devoted to God, in order to sacrifice them to the LORD your God at Gilgal." But Samuel replied: "Does the LORD delight in burnt offerings and sacrifices as much as in obeying the voice of the LORD? To obey is better than sacrifice, and to heed is better than the fat of rams." —1 Samuel 15:20–22

Saul had done a religious, good thing—brought out animals to be sacrificed to the Lord. And not just any animals, but the *best* animals. Yet God said Saul had sinned. Saul had obeyed the rules, as he interpreted them, but He had not obeyed the voice of the Lord. You see, God had told Saul to completely destroy everything and Saul had not responded to the Living Voice. His focus was the rules, not the Ruler.

The actions you take or refrain from taking because of God's present-tense voice are part of the praying life. Your obedience is prayer; it is a part of the interaction between the material realm and the spiritual realm. The same principle applies to the articulated aspect of prayer—saying prayer. The prayer of faith is the prayer authored by God. How is the Spirit of prayer in you moving you to pray? Until and unless you have more clear and specific leading, the prayer that releases all the power and provision of God is, "Let Your kingdom come in this situation; let Your will be done in this situation on earth the way Your will is done for this situation in heaven." Remember this: There is one name under heaven given among men that holds in it all the power, all the authority, all the riches of the spiritual realm. That name is Jesus. At the name of Jesus, all the power of God is released. The name of Jesus is the only prayer-word you need to know. As you become more familiar with the sound of His voice, you will begin to pray more details—if He chooses to reveal them to you. When you hear His voice, you are to *follow* Him. The most common tendency is to hear His voice and embellish it; to hear Him say one thing and then complete the thought for Him.

His voice is most likely going to be one step, not the whole picture. A person might sense God leading him to look into starting a business. That's all he knows. But his tendency will be to finish the thought—start a business and it will be very successful because God told me to do it. All God said was, "Look into starting a business." It may be that there is a person he needs to meet, or information he needs to have, or something in his flesh that needs to be exposed to him and the process of looking into starting a business will bring him into position for what God wants to do next. Do you see what I'm saying? You only know the step in front of you. Obey the one thing you know and wait to see what comes next.

In your current situation, what is the one thing you know? Write it out.

Have you obeyed the one thing you know, or are you waiting until you can see the bigger picture? What is stopping you from obeying the one thing you know?

Week 10, Day 5

<u>PRACTICE A NEW WAY OF PRAYING</u>

Darling child, you need to desire My will for the right purpose. You desperately want to know My will for the situation you are facing. You want Me to give you a detailed course of action. You think that if you could only know how and when, then you could have faith. But I will never do that because I am growing your capacity to trust Me. I am teaching you how to rely on your spiritual senses. I will show you the direction I am going, but not how I'll get there. Learn the adventure of watching My will unfold. — Jennifer Kennedy Dean, *Secret Place of the Most High*

_____

_____

_____

_____

_____

Week Ten Anniversary Thought

At the age of 20, I made an unreserved commitment of my life to Jesus Christ. I had made a genuine profession of faith many years before that, but I reached a juncture at which I had to decide the trajectory of my life. Would I be satisfied to follow the rules of my religion and mouth its doctrines correctly? Would I act out the roles cast for me by culture and tradition, which sometimes masquerade as righteousness? Or would I respond to this nagging sense of dissatisfaction that hinted at the possibility of something more? A steady drumbeat deep inside seemed to lure me to another path. I was being wooed by the Spirit's invitation: "Why do you seek the living among the dead?" And I could not resist.

During the years that have followed, I have passionately pursued a present-tense relationship with the living and indwelling Jesus. I have narrowed my goals to one goal for every moment that I live: to be completely and utterly abandoned to Him. I don't know where that will lead me; but wherever it leads me, that is where I'm going.

People often ask me, "What is your five-year plan?" My answer: "To be completely and utterly abandoned to Him." Long ago I learned that following the Ruler instead of the rules would take me down paths I could not have imagined. Every day I traverse new terrain, desperately dependent upon the moment-by-moment guidance of Jesus because He is leading me into new territory. He reminds me that my eyes must be fastened on Him, *"then you will know which way to go, since you have never been this way before"* (Joshua 3:4).

The danger I want to avoid is twofold. First, I don't want to impose pre-packaged beliefs handed down to me by human beings upon the pure truth of the living, active Word of the living, active God. Second, I don't want to depend on and put my faith in my ability to follow a set of religious rules that appear godly on the exterior, but are stuffed with flesh-based motivations. Do you realize that Jesus' detractors were the most religious men of the day? The men who most scrupulously followed all the laws and propounded only the most accepted theological thought? They were so carefully following the letter of the law that they missed the Spirit of the Law embodied in Jesus. They looked right into His face and did not see Him. His words fell upon their ears, but they did not hear Him (see John 8:42–43). I recoil at such a possibility. My heart cries, *"Show me your face, let me hear your voice; for your voice is sweet, and your face is lovely"* (Song of Solomon 2:14).

I am learning to live out a life fueled by faith. From the days when I took my first tentative baby steps, tripped, and fell and tried again, until along the way my steps have become steadier as I navigate the kingdom landscape, I have lived all these years in a faith lab. Every day I put faith to the test, and every day my walk becomes more confident and sure. I still trip and fall and get up and try again. Certainly I have much left to learn. If you are following a set of beliefs, you can finally learn them all. If you are following the Master, there is no end to the learning.

Leave behind tame, timid, play-it-safe, follow-the-rules faith. Learn to exercise an outrageous, get-out-of-the-boat, resurrection faith.

Obey and Forgive

DAY ONE

Dear friends, if our hearts do not condemn us, we have confidence before God and receive from him anything we ask, because we obey his commands and do what pleases him. —1 John 3:21–22

Obedience is essential for prayer. Once again, it is important to understand *why* obedience is essential to prayer. Obedience is not a trade-off: "I'll obey if You'll answer my prayer." We cannot buy the answers to our prayers with our actions. Obedience is not a way to get God in our debt so that He owes us something. Obedience is not a favor we do for God. To understand how obedience impacts prayer, let's put all the pieces together.

1. **Prayer is more than the words we say**; it is the total relationship in which we live; it is the ongoing interaction between the material and physical realms.
2. **Prayer begins with God** and achieves its true purpose when it is an expression of His heart.
3. **God has given us a set of spiritual senses** to hear Him and to "see" what the Father is doing, so that prayer will be effective and will produce results on the earth. Then we can access by prayer all that God wants to put on the earth.
4. **Disobedience dulls our spiritual senses**.

Disobedience does not change anything except our ability to perceive spiritual truth. If I were looking at something and I removed my contact lenses, it would not change anything about the situation except my ability to see it clearly. I would still be able to make out the vague outlines, but the details would elude me. In my praying life, this blurring would limit my power as an intercessor because I would not be able to see spiritual reality clearly. I would lose my ability to hear the subtle nuances of His communication. Jesus once said to His enemies, *"Why is my language not clear to you? Because you are unable to hear what I say"* (John 8:43). Do you see that a person can hear the words, but not hear the heart? I want to hear Him. I want to hear all the layers of His words. I want to know Him as intimately as possible. I don't want to miss out on anything He's doing. E. M. Bounds wrote, "God takes nothing by halves. He gives nothing by halves. We can have the whole of Him when He has the whole of us." I want all of Him! Is that true of you, too? Then let's look carefully at prayer and obedience.

Does obedience win God's favor and convince Him to act?

In your own words, what part does obedience play in prayer?

Week 11, Day 1

PRACTICE A NEW WAY OF PRAYING

"Speak, Lord, for your servant is listening." —1 Samuel 3:9

DAY TWO

Read some thoughts from God's Word about obedience and answer the following questions:

Read John 14:21. To whom will Jesus reveal Himself?

Read John 15:7. What is the key to answered prayer?

Read John 15:10 and 1 John 3:24. What keeps a believer abiding in Christ?

What was the standard of obedience Jesus called for from His disciples? What defines the obedience that will bring power in prayer? *"If you obey my commands, you will remain in my love, **just as I have obeyed my Father's commands** and remain in his love"* (John 15:10).

Expound on the phrase "just as I have obeyed my Father's commands." What do you think were some of the characteristics of Jesus' obedience?

What do you think Jesus means by the phrase, "you will remain in my love"? Does He mean that when you disobey He removes His love? Look at the following statements from God's Word to clarify this thought:

"Though the mountains be shaken and the hills be removed, yet my unfailing love for you will not be shaken nor my covenant of peace be removed," says the LORD, who has compassion on you. —Isaiah 54:10

If we are faithless, he will remain faithful, for he cannot disown himself. —2 Timothy 2:13

Will Jesus remove His love from you because of disobedience? No! Nothing can separate you from the love of God. He has settled His love on you. What, then, do you think Jesus means when He says, *"If you obey my commands, you will remain in my love, just as I have obeyed my Father's commands and remain in his love"* (John 15:10)?

The kind of obedience Jesus calls for—the kind of obedience that will attune our lives to the spiritual realm—goes beyond adherence to a set of rules. "If you obey Me the same way that I obey the Father," Jesus said. How did Jesus obey the Father?

He did nothing except in direct obedience to the Father.

He obeyed immediately.

He obeyed fully.

He was uncompromising in His obedience.

Jesus obeyed the Father as He heard Him in the moment. Jesus assures us that we can obey Him the same way that He obeyed the Father—in the moment. The starting point for this obedience to His present voice is in His law, or His commandments and statutes.

The Foundation of God's Will in His Law

One aspect of God's Word is His law. In His law we clearly encounter His will. In listening for His present voice, we do not ignore His written Word. We listen for His voice in His Word. As we give ourselves fully to obedience, we must begin in His law. One can view a lawgiver from two perspectives. First, there's the overbearing, power-hungry, demanding authority figure who says, "I'm laying down the law and you have to obey it because I'm the one with the power. I'm establishing a code of behavior that suits me, and I'm expecting you to follow my rules. If you don't, I'll punish you."

This is not God the lawgiver.

Here's God the lawgiver: "I'm the Creator. I made everything that exists. Because I love you, I'm giving you the laws of the universe. I'm telling you how to get the most out of all that I have created for you. I'm telling you the secrets about how things work so that you can live the life you are created for."

God is the lawgiver because God is the Creator.

God's will for you is that you flourish and prosper. His law is your protection and your wisdom. His law is encoded in your spiritual DNA so that in following it you are cooperating in establishing your own fulfillment and success.

DNA is an earth-picture that explains Spirit-truth. Your DNA is the instruction manual for your body. It tells each cell how to do its job. Everything about your physical structure is encoded in your DNA. Your DNA determines what size shoe you'll wear, what color your hair or eyes will be, how tall you'll grow. You will be unable to change anything prescribed by your DNA because it is structural. You can make cosmetic changes, but not structural ones. For example, you can dye your hair, but it will always grow out the color your DNA says it is.

God's law is encoded in your spiritual DNA. It is written in your heart. You cannot change it. He has built His law into the structure of human beings. In working against it, we are working against our own best interest. In resisting it, we resist peace and harmony. Outside His law, we are engaged in an ongoing, energy-draining, life-sapping upstream swim. In giving us His law, He has not restricted us, but freed us.

I run in the path of your commands, for you have set my heart free.... Direct me in the path of your commands, for there I find delight.
—Psalm 119:32, 35

The law of the LORD is perfect, reviving the soul.... The precepts of the LORD are right, giving joy to the heart. —Psalm 19:7–8

The psalmist writes of God's laws: "*By them is your servant warned; in keeping them there is great reward*" (Psalm 19:11). Do you see any areas of your life in which you are ignoring God's precepts? If so, do you realize that you are diminishing your life and diluting the power of your prayers?

Do you see that willful sin eventually enslaves you? Pray the words of Scripture: *"Keep your servant also from willful sins; may they not rule over me"* (Psalm 19:13). *"Direct my footsteps according to your word; let no sin rule over me"* (Psalm 119:133).

Do you acknowledge that disobedience will impair your spiritual senses by which you discern God's will? Make the following prayer your own.

Today's date:_____

Father, I open my life to You. Search me, know my thoughts. Try me, know my ways. Show me any wrong direction in my life. Put my feet back on Your path. I will settle for nothing less than all You have for me. Therefore, I forsake every wrong way. Lead me in the everlasting way. "I open my mouth and pant, longing for your commands" (Psalm 119:131). In Jesus' name.

❖

Week 11, Day 2

PRACTICE A NEW WAY OF PRAYING

"Speak, LORD, for your servant is listening." —1 Samuel 3:9

DAY THREE

"And when you stand praying, if you hold anything against anyone, forgive him, so that your Father in heaven may forgive you your sins" (Mark 11:25). Failing to forgive anyone for anything is closing the door to God. If we, as intercessors, are to be the channels of God's will into the world, we cannot clog the channels with anger and bitterness. Holding on to anger is cutting off the flow of His power through us. The Scripture tells us that unforgiveness gives the enemy, Satan, an opportunity to carry out his schemes: *"And what I have forgiven—if there was anything to forgive—I have forgiven in the sight of Christ for your sake, in order that Satan might not outwit us. For we are not unaware of his schemes"* (2 Corinthians 2:10–11).

Scripture teaches that nursing bitterness is:

a. a natural human reaction to pain and there is nothing you need to do about it.

b. something you can't help; something you are powerless against.

c. a sin.

God tells us that allowing bitterness to root and grow is a sin. Any action or attitude that causes you to miss out on the full glory of God—anything that causes you to be less than you were created to be—God calls "sin." He warns you away from sin because He longs for you to know His fullness and your full potential.

God hates sin because God loves you!

How does God expand on the word "sin" in this verse? "*For all have sinned and fall short of the glory of God*" (Romans 3:23). Sometimes we read this familiar verse (Romans 3:23) as if it said, "All have sinned and have fallen short of the expectations of God." We think of sin as having done something that caused God to be disappointed in us. Re-think it with me.

Can one be disappointed unless he expected something different? Is God surprised by our sin? Did He think we would be sinless, then experience disappointment when He discovered we weren't? Then, can we have disappointed Him? Can we have fallen short of His expectations?

What is "the glory of God"? The word "glory" in the Greek (*doxa*) can mean "the luster or the radiance of something: that which displays it." For example, you don't see the sun; you see the glory (radiance, outshining) of the sun. The purpose of human beings is to display the life of the Father—to be His "glory." Because of sin, we have fallen short of that destiny.

Romans 3:23 says that it is sin that keeps us from our destiny. It is sin that robs us of our birthright. It is sin that makes us less than our original design. Sin is your enemy, and that makes it God's enemy.

God will not come to terms or reach a compromise with His enemy. He will not settle for leaving "just a little bit" of sin to diminish your life. He is always rooting it out, exposing it, bringing it into the light. He wants you to forgive **everyone** for **everything** because He loves you obsessively and wants to see you reach your potential: the glory of God.

God, expressing Himself through Christ, is the model for how we are to forgive. "*Be kind and compassionate to one another, forgiving each other, just as in Christ God forgave you*" (Ephesians 4:32). How does God forgive?

1. **He forgives completely.** *"For I will forgive their wickedness and will remember their sins no more"* (Hebrews 8:12). *"And where these have been forgiven, there is no longer any sacrifice for sin"* (Hebrews 10:18).

2. **He forgives us when we didn't deserve it and didn't even desire it.** *"But God demonstrates his own love for us in this: While we were still sinners, Christ died for us"* (Romans 5:8).

3. **He began the forgiving process even while the offense was in progress.** *"When they came to the place called the Skull, there they crucified him, along with the criminals—one on his right, the other on his left. Jesus said, 'Father, forgive them, for they do not know what they are doing.' And they divided up his clothes by casting lots"* (Luke 23:33–34).

Is there any person whose offense you need to forgive?

*"And when you stand praying, if you hold **anything** against **anyone**, forgive him, so that your Father in heaven may forgive you your sins."* —Mark 11:25

*"Forgive us our sins, for we also forgive **everyone** who sins against us."* —Luke 11:4

Write out your commitment: Right now, today, I choose to forgive _____ and to cancel his or her debt against me. I choose to be free of the bitterness that poisons my life and keeps me tethered to the past.

Week 11, Day 3

PRACTICE A NEW WAY OF PRAYING

"Speak, Lord, for your servant is listening." —1 Samuel 3:9

_____

_____

_____

_____

_____

_____

_____

DAY FOUR

Read the following excerpt from my book, *Heart's Cry*:

Every act of obedience is a step toward greater freedom. For example, Jesus said, *"When you stand praying. if you hold anything against anyone, forgive him"* (Mark 11:25). This is a difficult thing to obey because our spiritual genetics predispose us to hold a grudge or exact revenge. The command to forgive everyone for everything opposes our human nature. The command to forgive seems like a heavy burden to bear. It seems too much to ask.

Having heard the command of Christ, you are now faced with a choice. Will you be a slave to anger and bitterness, which will lead to your own destruction? Or will you forgive and be freed from the too-heavy, emotionally crippling burden of anger? Will you draw on the resources of the kingdom of the world or will you draw on the resources of the kingdom of God? You choose.

I want to explore the issue of forgiveness further because it is a command directly tied to prayer. There are many levels of offense, all of which must be forgiven for your own good. However, I know that some of you who are reading this book have been betrayed or abused and are suffering great inner pain. That pain may be intensified by feelings of guilt brought on by knowing you should be able to forgive. Remember several things.

Forgiveness is a process. It is not accomplished by saying a few magic words. It is a process initiated and completed by Christ in you. You do not have a deadline to meet. Your process may be different from anyone else's. You may be encouraged or guided by the similar experiences of others, but don't be dictated to by them. Be patient with yourself. Remember that God has undertaken the work within you and the responsibility is His. Once you have entered the process by yielding yourself to His working, you have fulfilled His commandment.

You can't begin the process until you can face your anger and hurt honestly. Let me quote from Carole E. Smith, M.S., M.A., of the Atlanta Counseling Center:

"We cannot know God fully until we know who we are and what has formed us. We do not go to God despite the sin perpetrated upon us. We go to God because of it, and we must take it to God held in both hands, known by heart and seen with both eyes. That is when we can hand it over. That is when we can forgive our abusers.

"Yet, many Christians today seem intent on stressing that there is a quicker route to God, that there are steps that will lift us up and over sin and pain, that we can pray and forgive another without ever knowing or examining the imprint that sin had on our lives. Such is resurrection without crucifixion. It is Bonhoeffer's 'cheap grace': a magic carpet to recovery that sounds right but never gets off the ground."

Don't be afraid to take your pain and anger to God. He won't reject you. He is not fragile. You can ask Him your hardest questions. You can lay your blackest anger before Him, even when some of that anger is directed at Him. He will take you by the hand and walk you step by step through the process of forgiveness and inner healing. He will put all the pieces back together again. As He does, He will show you Himself in new and glorious ways. He will use even the most awful events for your good. Your pain and the subsequent healing and transformation will make you into a powerful intercessor.

In your own words, how does forgiveness bring freedom?

Are you carrying a grudge against someone right now? Look at it in the full light of His presence. How is it crippling you? Where is it holding you back?

Ask Him to show you how to forgive. Begin now, in His power, the process of forgiving. That might mean looking squarely at the pain for the first time. Are you willing to walk through the process with Him?

Week 11, Day 4

PRACTICE A NEW WAY OF PRAYING

"Speak, LORD, for your servant is listening." —1 Samuel 3:9

DAY FIVE

Consider further the process you have entered into—the process of forgiving. This process is likely to lead through some hard truths. You will probably have to face some unpleasant realizations about yourself. But don't be afraid. This is a cleansing, freeing process. Where sin is evident, grace is all the more present and powerful. He came not for the healthy, but for the ailing; not for the strong, but for the weak. In the spiritual realm, your weakness is an asset!

Consider the following Scripture verses:

Jesus answered them, "It is not the healthy who need a doctor, but the sick. I have not come to call the righteous, but sinners to repentance."
—Luke 5:31–32

But where sin increased, grace increased all the more. —Romans 5:20

If I must boast, I will boast of the things that show my weakness.
—2 Corinthians 11:30

But he said to me, "My grace is sufficient for you, for my power is made perfect in weakness." Therefore I will boast all the more gladly about my weaknesses, so that Christ's power may rest on me. —2 Corinthians 12:9

Before you begin to look at hard truths about yourself and about your own sin, write in your own words how God views your weaknesses and vulnerabilities. Why does He need for you to face and recognize your own flesh?

Look at the grudge you have been holding on to—the one you are in the process of forgiving. You've already looked at the pain inflicted on you by the perpetrator of the wrong. Now look at what aspect of the self-principle is impacted by this hurtful act or attitude toward you. What is it in you that responds to the hurt? Read and reflect on these passages from my book, *Secret Place of the Most High*:

Offspring of My Spirit, bitterness is not at home in you. I indwell you, and your life is not the natural environment for bitterness to root and grow. It is a weed, a fruit destroyer, and invader. It is sapping your joy and stunting your growth. Let Me have it all and I will uproot it. Unable to receive nourishment, it will wither and die. You will be free. Give me your permission to begin the process.

My well-watered garden, I am beginning My uprooting project by digging underneath the root. Let Me show you what I found there. Give attention to Me while I shovel out the muck that nourished the root of bitterness. What made the offense offensive? What unhealed wound did it touch? What unsurrendered pain did it awaken? What insecurity did it unmask? What uncrucified flesh did it discover?

What does the offense or the hurt touch in you? Is it pride? Is it insecurity? Is it a misplaced focus? Think through these truths and build an understanding of how God can use the hurt you have suffered to strengthen you in His Spirit and to flush out the lingering self-life that is alive in you, disguised and hidden.

1. It is not wrong to feel hurt and even anger at an offense.
2. It is wrong to let that hurt or anger take up residence in you and receive nourishment to grow and get strong. It is wrong because it diminishes you and slows your progress.
3. Immediately, at the moment of an offense, turn it toward God as His opportunity to free you further from the dead weight of your self-life. Let Him use the hurt to expose sin's devious strongholds and tear them down.
4. Recognize that sin's power lies in being undetected. When it is exposed to the Light, God can begin to cleanse you from that unrighteousness.

<u>PRACTICE A NEW WAY OF PRAYING</u>

"Speak, Lord, for your servant is listening." —1 Samuel 3:9

_____

_____

_____

_____

_____

Week Eleven Anniversary Thought

Allow me to share something about the freedom of obedience from a journal I kept during my husband's illness.

Today as I sat beside Wayne's hospital bed, I watched a parable in action.

Wayne is being fed and medicated by IV right now. Lots of tubes acting as the conduit through which life and healing flow. Wayne is very restless. He keeps moving his arm in such a way that the IV lines get tangled and the healing flow can't get to him. When he starts moving his arm too much, we have to take his hand and gently hold it down so he won't get the lines tangled. It frustrates him. He feels we are restricting his freedom. He is missing the context. All he knows is he wants his hand to move and we want it to be still. He can't see that what he thinks is restriction is really freedom—freedom to receive the flow that sustains his life.

Like Wayne, we often chafe at God's call to obedience, thinking it restricts us. Our view is narrow. We can't see that His loving hand on ours is freedom. It keeps us in the place where His power and provision flow. It keeps us from moving out of the flow of His life.

This morning when I got to Wayne's room, they had tied that restless hand to the bed with just enough give that he had freedom, but not license. In other words, he could move his hand, but only within the confines of that which was safe for him. It was a comfortable, soft little cuff around his wrist, but it surprised me and hurt me when I saw it.

I thought, how much better when the discipline comes from a loving hand. How much better when that "restriction" is accompanied with a loving touch and gentle words instead of in an impersonal "law" that has no heart. See how much God loves us? His guidance comes to us from His loving hand, accompanied by His gentle voice, until we learn by experience that His commands set us free.

"I will run in the path of your commands, for you have set my heart free" (Psalm 119:32).

Authority in Prayer

DAY ONE

God does not teach us to pray from a position of weakness. We will be in a position of weakness in ourselves, but in the spiritual realm we are in a position of authority. He gives us the authority to activate His will on earth; the authority to bring His power into situations on earth. The proof that we are to pray with authority is that we have been authorized to use the name of Jesus. The One who has all authority in heaven and on earth has authorized us to speak in His name.

When one person gives another the privilege of using his or her name, it is an indication of trust. It is saying to another, "Use the credibility I have earned to establish your own. You will not need to prove yourself in order to have immediate access to the benefits I have earned because you will be coming in my name and not your own. My reputation will be imputed to you. You will be received as I am."

My parents are wonderful people and I benefit from their reputation. When I meet someone who has known my parents, that person immediately begins to treat me with a respect I have not earned. The person treats me with the respect he or she has for my parents. The reputation my parents have earned is imputed to me. I am treated as if I had actually done all the generous and loving things my parents have done simply because I bear their name.

This is the privilege Jesus has given us. We approach the Father in His name. When we pray in Jesus' name, the whole spiritual realm must deploy accordingly. Let's think first about the power in the Name. Tomorrow we will see what it means to use the Name.

Before we even begin to use our inadequate little words to describe the power in the Name, would you stop and ask the Spirit of Truth to guide you into all truth about the Name? I can't even think about the Name without being overwhelmed with its majesty and its power. I am so awed at the Name that I want to be sure you see its holiness and my words certainly will not convey it. Unless the Spirit of God Himself shows you the Name, you will never understand it. Stop now and ask Him to teach you.

Learning the Name

When I was expecting my first child, it occurred to me that I would have a new name, a name I had never been called before. For the first time, someone would call me Mommy. Even though billions of women have the same name, the name Mommy would still be entirely unique and my own because it named the relationship between me and my child. Even though billions of women are Mommy to someone, only I would be Mommy to Brantley Quin Dean.

As I considered this monumental change in my life, I began to worry. "How will my child learn my name? Since no one else calls me Mommy, how will he know to? Why won't he call me what everyone else calls me? How will he come to understand that the unique and intimate relationship he and I will share entitles me to be called Mommy?"

I reached this conclusion: I'll have to tell him my name. I'll have to teach him my new name. I'll have to weave it into his life, identifying it with his experience of me. As we interact, as we bond, as we learn each other, I'll teach him my name. That's the only way Brantley Quin Dean will know my name.

Of course, Mommy is not my legal name. Mommy is only my name to my children. It would be silly for anyone else to call me Mommy, because I'm only Mommy to Brantley, Kennedy, and Stinson. To them, that's my name because to them, that's my relationship. When they were little and we were in a place with other little children, sometimes I would hear the cry, "Mommy!" I would look around to see who was saying it. If it was not my child, then it was not my name being called. Mommy is the name that defines my role in their lives.

In the same way, God has carefully and patiently taught us His name, the name that defines the relationship, the name that explains the bond. He introduced Himself to Moses. "Whom shall I tell them sent me?" Moses asked the voice from the burning bush. "Tell them I AM has sent you," the voice answered.

In this way, God begins to teach His children His name. God's name is too big, His investment in us too far-reaching, His love for us too boundless to be packaged in one word. So He first gives an open-ended name. I AM. He leaves room for our understanding of Him and of our relationship to Him to expand. He grows our knowledge of His name with each encounter. He weaves it into our experience of Him. We continue to learn new parts of His name as we continue to learn new truths about His ways. Each new piece of His name that He teaches us introduces us to a new aspect of our relationship to Him. "This is who I am to you," He is saying. "This is what our relationship entitles you to call Me."

He progressively reveals His name. Little by little, encounter by encounter, He teaches His name.

The Name is too big to be spoken by human lips or contained in one word. God taught us His name bit by bit. Throughout the Old Testament, God revealed His name as He intervened in the lives of His people. One time He calls Himself "The Lord Who Provides," another time He says His name is "The Lord Who Makes You Holy," and yet another time He calls Himself "The Lord Who Heals You." He continues to reveal His name throughout history until Jesus is born on the earth. Little by little, encounter by encounter, He teaches us His name.

Imagine that you were a creature from another galaxy who came to earth to study its landscape and climate. You land on earth and begin to transmit your findings. Would those findings be accurate? How you described the earth would depend on what part of the planet you landed on and what time of year you landed there. You could not possibly describe the earth from one place. God is bigger than the earth. One view of Him, one simple definition of Him, will not even begin to define Him. He has to teach us His name a little at a time. Many Jews, out of reverence and the understanding that one word will not say the whole name, call God *Ha-shem*, which means "The Name."

The Name in all its forms has been consolidated into one name: Jesus.

The Name in all its forms has been consolidated into one name: Jesus. God gave Him the Name. "*Holy Father, protect them by the power of your name—the name you gave me,*" Jesus prayed in John 17:11.

Therefore God exalted him to the highest place and gave him the name that is above every name, that at the name of Jesus every knee should bow, in heaven and on earth and under the earth, and every tongue confess that Jesus Christ is Lord, to the glory of God the Father. —Philippians 2:9–11

When His people speak His name, all the forces in the spiritual realm have to deploy accordingly. "*God exalted him to the highest place and gave him the name that is above every name,*" Paul writes. Is this present-tense truth, or future-tense truth? Is Jesus already exalted to the highest place? Is He already the name above every name? Look at Ephesians 1:20–21. Paul has described finished work—a work that is completed and available in the spiritual realm, or the "heavenlies."

What is God's reason for exalting Jesus and giving Him the name above all names? The Scripture says it is so that "*at the name of Jesus every knee should bow, in heaven and on earth and under the earth, and every tongue confess that Jesus Christ is Lord to the glory of God the Father.*" Is this present-tense truth, or future-tense truth? It is present tense! It is true now and will continue to be true throughout eternity. Right now, at the name of Jesus, every knee in the spiritual realm bows—if not in worship, then in surrender— and every tongue in the spiritual realm has to confess (agree with; admit) the lordship of Jesus and become subject to the authority of Jesus. The phrase "should bow" does not mean "ought to bow." The word "should" means "implying necessity in accordance with the nature of things or with the divine appointment and therefore certain, destined to take place." At the name of Jesus, it is necessary in accordance with the nature of things—it is certain to take place—every knee bows and tongue confesses His lordship. It is a present-tense reality in the spiritual realm— the name of Jesus stops the forces of Satan cold.

The Name is not contained in the word formed by the letters J-e-s-u-s. The Name is not the sound that our voices make when we say the word "Jesus." Many people have been and still are named Jesus. The name does not exalt the person; the person exalts the name.

The word "J-e-s-u-s" is our code word for the Name. When we say the name of Jesus with reverence, when we speak it of the Son of God, the Prince of Peace, Lord and Savior, then it reverberates through the spiritual realm as the Name. The forces of evil tremble and fall on their faces; the warriors of the Lord snap to attention; the angels are on alert. The cry goes out: "The Name has been exalted. Someone spoke the Name." Heaven acts when God's people speak the Name.

"*Until now you have not asked for anything in my name,*" Jesus said to His disciples in John 16:24. "*Ask and you will receive, and your joy will be complete.*" When we ask in His name, all of the resources of heaven are ours to use in bringing glory to the Father. "*I will do whatever you ask in my name, so that the Son may bring glory to the Father. You may ask me for anything in my name, and I will do it*" (John 14:13–14).

As an experience of worship, bow before Him (physically or mentally) and exalt the Name. Speak the name of Jesus reverently. Sing songs that exalt His name. Let the Spirit lead you in honoring the Name. Be very conscious that every prayer you pray is in the name of Jesus. Let your mind dwell on everything that means.

Ask the Spirit, whose job it is to lead you into all truth, to reveal to you the power in the Name. Take a request—one that is urgent for you right now—and let the Spirit show you how to take it to the Father in the name of the Son. Write out what it means to you right now to pray for that request in Jesus' name.

Week 12, Day 1

<u>PRACTICE A NEW WAY OF PRAYING</u>

As you remember your needs and your desires that you are bringing to God in prayer, limit your prayer vocabulary to one word: *Jesus.*

DAY TWO

What does it mean to use the name of Jesus in prayer? We are to use His name to access His resources to fulfill His purposes through prayer. His one purpose is to glorify the Father.

The power in prayer is from the Spirit, but the authority in prayer is from Jesus. Authority and power are different. Power is ability; authority is the legal right. A person with authority is the one who has been authorized. I may have the ability (power) to drive a car, but if I do not have the authority (legal right), then I cannot do it.

Imagine a traffic policeman standing in the middle of a busy intersection directing traffic. Now imagine a huge semi barreling toward that intersection. When the policeman holds up his hand, signaling the semi to come to a halt, the semi will obey. Which has more power—the semi or the policeman? The semi does, of course. But which one has authority? The policeman does. Because of his authority, the policeman can bring the semi to a screeching halt just by holding up his hand! Because of the name of Jesus, you have the authority to pray with power.

When we use the Name in prayer, it has two effects. First, it gives us access to the Father. Because Jesus has given us permission to use His name, we are received in the Father's presence as Jesus is. We lay aside our own unworthiness and clothe ourselves in Jesus.

The union that empowers to the use of the Name may be the union of love. When a bride whose life has been one of poverty becomes united to the bridegroom, she gives up her own name, to be called by his, and has now the full right to use it. She purchases in his name, and that name is not refused. And this is done because the bridegroom has chosen her for himself, counting on her to care for his interests: they are now one. And so the Heavenly Bridegroom could do nothing less; having loved us and made us one with Himself, what could He do but give those who bear His Name the right to present it before the Father, or to come with it to Himself for all they need.... The bearing of the name of another supposes my having given up my own and with it my own independent life; but then, as surely, my possession of all there is in the name I have taken instead of my own.
—Andrew Murray, *With Christ in the School of Prayer*

This is perhaps the most amazing thing of all: When I embraced the lordship of Jesus over my life, He became my life. Now, I am "*in Him*" (Ephesians 1:13) and He is "*in me*" (Colossians 3:3). My union with Him is the same as His union with the Father: "*Just as you are in me and I am in you,*" Jesus prayed in John 17:21. When the Father looks at me, He no longer sees Jennifer and Jesus, two separate beings; He sees Jesus in His Jennifer-form. When I come to the Father in the name of Jesus, it is not a formality; it is a reality. He hears my prayers through the voice of Jesus. That is the power of the Name.

Second, when you use the name of Jesus, you immediately have authority in the spiritual realm. The "heavenlies," the active spiritual realm, respond to the Name. Keeping in mind that prayer is not simply asking God for things, but instead is a continual interaction with the spiritual realm, using the name of Jesus in prayer gives you the authority to declare to rulers and authorities in the heavenly realms what the manifold wisdom of God is (Ephesians 3:10). Your prayers in Jesus' name—which means that you are speaking His desires—direct the will of God into the circumstances of earth. Read what O. Hallesby says about accessing the power of God for situations on earth:

This power is so rich and so mobile that all we have to do when we pray is to point to the persons or things to which we desire to have this power applied, and He, the Lord of this power, will direct the necessary power to the desired place at once.

He has decreed that only His own friends can establish contact with these inexhaustible sources of power. In fact, the means of contact has been devised so carefully that the connection is automatically cut off, even to the friends of Jesus, as soon as they try to employ this power in ways contrary to the will and purposes of Jesus. It is only when we pray for something according to the will of God that we have the promise of being heard and answered. —O. Hallesby, *Prayer*

List some situations in which you use someone else's name to establish your credibility.

When you use someone else's name, do you receive the treatment you deserve, or the treatment reserved for the person in whose name you are coming?

When a person gives you permission to use his or her name, what is the trust implied?

In your own words, what does it mean to pray in Jesus' name?

When you use the name of Jesus, you are exercising the authority to direct the will of God into the circumstances of earth. When Jesus gave His prayer outline, He included in it this phrase: "*Your kingdom come, your will be done on earth as it is in heaven*" (Matthew 6:10). He uses here a language construct that is used to give command. He is not saying, "Oh, please, Father. I'm hoping that Your kingdom will come and that Your will will be done." He is saying, "Come, kingdom. Be done, will of God." He is bringing the will of God and the rule of God into situations on earth by means of prayer. When you pray in His name, you are doing the same thing.

He is not commanding God! Don't get confused here. He is not demanding that God act. He is announcing to the spiritual realm that the will of God *will be done* and that the rule of God *will take effect*. We will begin tomorrow to look at the restrictions on this authority given to us through the name of Jesus.

Week 12, Day 2

PRACTICE A NEW WAY OF PRAYING

As you remember your needs and your desires that you are bringing to God in prayer, limit your prayer vocabulary to one word: *Jesus*.

DAY THREE

The authority we have in Christ is *delegated* authority. Let's carefully examine the Scripture to see how delegated authority operates and how it differs from original authority. We use our delegated authority—we use His name—to access His riches to fulfill His purposes through prayer.

Read John 14:13–14. What is always Jesus' primary purpose?

❖

When we pray in Jesus' name, we will bring into the situation the resources and the timing and the events that will most clearly display God's power and will glorify His name. Praying in Jesus' name does not ensure that situations will be resolved in the way and in the time that you expect. You do not influence God to do your will; you influence the spiritual realm to do God's will. God knows how to glorify Himself.

Let me repeat how delegated authority works: We use His name to access His riches to fulfill His purposes through prayer. Let me illustrate this way: I am president of a certain organization. As president, I must sign all checks written on the organization's account. The organization has delegated authority to me for this purpose. By signing a check, I have the authority to access the organization's resources. However, I do not have the authority to decide where those resources will be applied. When I sign a check to release resources, it is for the purpose of applying those resources where the organization has determined they should be applied. I do not have the authority to access the organization's resources for my own benefit, or for any purposes except those set forth and approved by the membership. My signature releases the organization's resources to carry out the organization's plans. I act in the name of that organization. If I do not exercise the authority delegated to me—if I do not sign checks—the organization's purposes will not be accomplished. Similarly, Jesus has delegated authority to us to access His resources for His purposes. Our God-authored prayers release His riches just as the signature on a check releases the resources in that checking account. *Delegated authority is only in effect when it exactly matches the original authority that backs it up.*

There are two types of authority: original and delegated. Original authority means that authority is inherent. The person with original authority actually owns the authority—he is not exercising it on someone else's behalf. In the spiritual realm only Jesus has original authority. Let's look at His authority in the spiritual realm.

Read the following passages. Underline words and phrases that indicate the scope of Jesus' authority.

Then Jesus came to them and said, "All authority in heaven and on earth has been given to me." —Matthew 28:18

And God placed all things under his feet and appointed him to be head over everything for the church, which is his body, the fullness of him who fills everything in every way. —Ephesians 1:22–23

Therefore God exalted him to the highest place and gave him the name that is above every name, that at the name of Jesus every knee should bow, in heaven and on earth and under the earth, and every tongue confess that Jesus Christ is Lord, to the glory of God the Father. —Philippians 2:9–11

For by him all things were created: things in heaven and on earth, visible and invisible, whether thrones or powers or rulers or authorities; all things were created by him and for him. He is before all things, and in him all things hold together. And he is the head of the body, the church; he is the beginning and the firstborn from among the dead, so that in everything he might have the supremacy. —Colossians 1:16–18

How much authority does Jesus have? Is anything or anyone at all, outside His authority? Write out a statement describing the scope of His authority.

The authority that we exercise in prayer flows from Him. It is His authority. Actually, you and I do not have authority. We exercise His authority. Any time that our prayers are outside His will, they have no authority. Let me illustrate the way that original and delegated authority work together.

The president of the United States has original authority. Decisions originate with him. The Constitution of the United States gives him this authority (legal right). The secretary of state has delegated authority. The secretary of state negotiates with world leaders and hammers out treaties and agreements with other countries in the president's name. He has full authority to speak for the president as long as he is speaking the president's thoughts, as long as he is being the president's mouthpiece. Were the secretary of state to begin speaking his own thoughts as a private citizen, voicing his own ideas in his own name, he would no longer be speaking with authority. His authority is delegated. It must be backed up by original authority. Delegated authority is only operative when it is the exact representation of the original authority that backs it up.

Let me give you another example. As a volunteer, I teach writing workshops for elementary school children. One day I was teaching a writing workshop for 165 fourth-graders. I was having difficulty because I had no authority over them; they were not subject to me. My words had no effect on them because I had no authority. If I told them to be quiet, it was as if I hadn't spoken. My words had no power because I had no authority. At one point, the principal walked by and noticed my problem. She came into the room and sat where the children could see her. Suddenly the situation changed. Now those fourth-graders were subject to me. Now they obeyed every word I said. Why? Because the principal, the original authority, had delegated her authority to me. Because of her presence, the children responded to my words as if she had spoken them. I exercised her authority. It was as if her words were in my mouth. Delegated authority is just as effective as original authority as long as it exactly matches the original authority.

Actually, you and I do not have authority. We exercise His authority. Any time that our prayers are outside His will, they have no authority.

Jesus has given us delegated authority backed up by His original authority.

Our Lord said: "If ye shall ask anything in my name, I will do it" (John 14:14); but it is important to remember that all prayer in His name is prayer initiated, controlled, and directed by Him, not our own desires and petitions, but His desires and petitions made known to us, brought to the cognizance of our thoughts, so that we think them too. Only when we know and share in desires of the Lord Jesus Christ, can we really pray in His name, and not in our own.
—Hannah Hurnard, *God's Transmitters*

Can you pray with authority unless you pray in Jesus' name?

Can you pray in Jesus' name if you are not praying Jesus' desires?

When you and I pray the will and desires of Jesus, it is as if Jesus Himself is asking. Does the Father ever refuse the Son anything He asks? Look at John 11:41–42.

What do you think is the key to praying with authority?

Week 12, Day 3

PRACTICE A NEW WAY OF PRAYING

As you remember your needs and your desires that you are bringing to God in prayer, limit your prayer vocabulary to one word: *Jesus.*

_____

_____

_____

_____

_____

DAY FOUR

Prayer in Jesus' name enforces the authority and lordship of Jesus. Look at it like this: The United States has a government built on laws. No citizen of the United States is above the law. The law is the authority. As a citizen of the United States, its laws have authority over me; I am subject to them. The law says that I must drive no faster than 70 miles per hour (mph) on interstate highways. I am subject to that law. Does that mean that I can't drive any faster than 70 mph on interstate highways? Of course not; I can drive as fast as I want to drive. The law will only impact my specific situation if someone with authority enforces it—puts force behind it.

Jesus is Lord. We don't make Him Lord. He is Lord. Everything is subject to Him. Our prayers do a work in the spiritual realm that enforces (puts force behind) His lordship, bringing it to bear on a specific situation.

Elijah is cited as a man who prayed with authority. We looked in detail at Elijah as a prayer-model during Week Three. You may want to go back and review that material. James 5:17 reminds us that Elijah was only human—he was "a man just like us." Yet Elijah's prayers held rain off the earth for three and a half years, then brought rain back to the earth. James makes it clear: It was the prayer of Elijah that kept rain from the earth and returned rain to the earth. The power was God's; the plan was God's; the purpose was God's; but it was Elijah's prayer that caused God's will to be enforced on the earth. The prayer of a righteous man—like Elijah—exercises force, has effect, and creates change. Prayer enforces the lordship of Jesus, causing His rule to take direct effect.

Where did Elijah's authority originate? "*As the L*ORD*, the God of Israel lives, before whom I stand…*" was how Elijah stated His position (1 Kings 17:1 NASB).

God intends for prayer to change the earth. When we pray earth-changing prayers, we are to pray them with authority and boldness as Elijah, a man just like us, did. The authority we have in prayer is the authority to bind or loose that which has already been bound or loosed in heaven. When Elijah prayed rain off the earth, it was because God had proclaimed it so. When Elijah's prayers loosed rain on the earth, it was because God had proclaimed it so. We have the authority to proclaim God's will: "*Your kingdom come. Your will be done on earth as it is in heaven.*"

Complete the following statement that Jesus made concerning prayer in His name from John 14:13–14.

"And I will do _____ in my name, so
that the Son _____.
You may ask me for _____in my name, and I
will do it."

❖

Week 12, Day 4

PRACTICE A NEW WAY OF PRAYING

**As you remember your needs and your desires that you are bringing to God in prayer,
limit your prayer vocabulary to one word:** *Jesus.*

_____

_____

_____

_____

_____

DAY FIVE

The longer we live a praying life, the more focused we are on Him. The secret to powerful praying is not a method, but a relationship. Little by little we are freed from the uncertainty induced by scrutinizing our prayer methods to see if they measure up. Did I have enough faith? Did I pray fervently enough, or long enough, or eloquently enough? Did I present my case with enough passion? In the praying life, we can forget the method and look to the Master. The secret to prayer lies in Him alone.

Catherine Marshall shares what the Holy Spirit taught her as she was learning to pray with power. She made a chart and put on one side "My Effort" and on the other side "God's Response." One of her entries looks like this:

My Effort	God's Response
Tried to have faith in faith and work up faith by positive thinking, affirmations, and picturing.	He showed me this is putting faith in technique rather than in a Person–Jesus.

One of the most important lessons our Prayer Tutor will teach us is how to focus all of our faith on Him. As the Father brings your focus back to Him, you begin to see the integrated picture, all of reality as one truth. There are two sides to prayer, one seeming to contradict the other.

God's Sovereignty	My Choice
Your eyes saw my unformed body. All the days ordained for me were written in your book before one of them came to be. —Psalm 139:16	May he give you the desire of your heart and make all your plans succeed. —Psalm 20:4
The lot is cast into the lap, but its every decision is from the Lord. —Proverbs 16:33	You have granted him the desire of his heart and have not withheld the request of his lips. —Psalm 21:2
The LORD Almighty has sworn, "Surely, as I have planned, so it will be, and as I have purposed, so it will stand." —Isaiah 14:24	Delight yourself in the LORD and he will give you the desires of your heart. —Psalm 37:4
"For I know the plans I have for you," declares the LORD, "plans to prosper you and not to harm you, plans to give you hope and a future." —Jeremiah 29: 11	"He fulfills the desires of those who fear him; he hears their cry and saves them. —Psalm 145:19

In the praying life, the seeming contradictions are resolved. Here's how Oswald Chambers puts it in his book, *Christian Disciplines*: "The Holy Spirit not only brings us into the zone of God's influence but into intimate relationship with Him personally, so that by the slow discipline of prayer the choices of our free will become the preordinations of His almighty order."

Powerful praying occurs when:

1. I allow Him to align my thoughts and purposes with His.

2. I give up my preconceived ideas of what I want and need and allow Him to fill me with His abundance.

3. I bring my will into active cooperation with His.

4. My mind, will, and emotions become the conduits through which He can express His thoughts, desires, and longings.

"Draw near, My child," is Your sweet call. My heart yearns to enter into Your beckoning light. The services I have performed for You, the

rituals to ensure Your favor, have left me empty. I can't seem to get beyond the veil, where the alluring brightness of Your glory shines.

Rest, abide. These are the mysteries. Your works won't show the way. Look to My Son. He is the open door into My presence.

Lose yourself in Him to find your way to Me. *"See, I have placed before you an open door that no one can shut"* (**Revelation 3:8**).

—Jennifer Kennedy Dean, *Heart's Cry*

Week 12, Day 5

<u>PRACTICE A NEW WAY OF PRAYING</u>

As you remember your needs and your desires that you are bringing to God in prayer, limit your prayer vocabulary to one word: *Jesus*.

❖

Week Twelve Anniversary Thought

Let me take this opportunity to caution you about some readily available teaching on spiritual authority. Repeating some of this week's material, let me emphasize: You do not have authority. Jesus has authority.

You will not learn how to exercise your delegated authority by saying certain words in your prayers, or by praying louder or longer, or by working into an emotional state. You will know how your authority operates by spending much time with Jesus, letting Him imprint His heart upon yours.

Some would lead you to believe that you can demand whatever you want or whatever you decide is best because you have authority in prayer. That kind of teaching feeds right into the flesh's desire to run the show. Some might use phrases about the name of Jesus and the blood of Jesus, but prayer is not about phraseology. Authority is inherent in true, God-authored prayer no matter what words you use. Authority in prayer comes from surrender to Jesus.

Section Four

The Practice of Prayer

The Practice of Prayer

PRACTICE A NEW WAY OF PRAYING

This week, use the prayer of Thomas à Kempis: "What Thou wilt; as Thou wilt; when Thou wilt." Pray this prayer many times through the day as situations arise.

DAY ONE

The pursuit of any goal requires a narrowed focus. To hold fast to one goal means to dismiss many others. The pursuit of any goal demands a single-minded diligence. We must be willing to sacrifice anything not related to the firmly established goal. In the pursuit of God, we must evaluate life, not in terms of right or wrong but, "Does this push me toward my goal or distract me from my goal?" As God works to reproduce His heart in us, we will find that many things that are not technically "wrong" are still encumbrances that keep us from effectively running toward the goal. We find within ourselves the desire to divest ourselves of anything that may slow our progress. What may seem all right for a more casual seeker will be forbidden to us.

The more you experience seeing the power of God released in response to your prayers, the more excitement you have about prayer. If you are available to the Spirit at all times, He will bring many lives and needs to you for intercession. It will become your life's focus to see God work in every situation with tremendous power. Then you begin to realize that the more pure your life is, the more effectively it conducts the power of God. You begin to seek purity and obedience; they become qualities you desire in your life. You welcome God's purifying work because you know it is freeing you of encumbrances. In your heart, Jesus begins to reproduce His prayer: *"For their sakes I sanctify Myself"* (John 17:19 NASB). You will realize that to find power, you must seek purity. *"Blessed are the pure in heart, for they will see God"* (Matthew 5:8).

Take a minute to focus on the lives and situations God has brought to you for intercession. Do you long for your praying to be effective and powerful? Write down the names of people for whom you are praying and let the Spirit of Christ in you author this prayer: "For their sakes I sanctify myself."

As your life becomes a praying life, willingly, joyfully, we lay aside every weight. In 2 Peter 1:3 we read that He *called us by his own glory and goodness."* As we see more of His glory, as we experience more of His goodness, that in itself entices us and draws us to Him. The One who is calling us is so compelling that our sacrifice feels like privilege.

As a child, I always loved to go barefoot in the summer. I remember playing ball with my siblings and neighbors in our front yard. The rule was that we took turns chasing the ball into the street when it went astray. Every time my turn came to chase the ball into the street, I said, "I can't! I don't have any shoes on. The pavement will burn my feet!" So I never had to take my turn chasing the ball into the street.

My dad used to walk to and from his office every day and as he walked, he whistled. When I was in the yard playing ball (but unable to run into the street to retrieve it when it was my turn) often I'd hear my dad whistling. I knew he was on his way home. So off I'd go, running barefoot across the hot pavement, to meet him and walk the rest of the way home with him. When the outcome was sufficiently attractive, the discomfort involved was irrelevant. I wouldn't burn my feet for a ball, but I'd not even feel the pain if it meant extra time with my daddy.

The pursuit of any goal requires a narrowed focus. Choosing to live a praying life—a life through which the power of God is free to flow—involves sacrifice. In this, it is no different from any other rock-solid commitment. Whatever you choose to pursue will mean that you sacrifice something else. The key is this: If the goal is sufficiently attractive, the sacrifice required will be irrelevant. In fact, the more focused on your goal you are, the less you will perceive the requirements as "sacrifices."

When my son Stinson was a toddler, I picked him up from a birthday party he had attended. He came out proudly clutching a red helium-filled balloon. "Stinson, what a wonderful balloon!" I said. "Don't let go of it or it will go way up in the sky and we won't be able to get it back."

I turned around for a moment, and when I turned back, there was Stinson, watching his wonderful red helium-filled balloon float higher and higher. "Oh, I'm sorry you lost your balloon, Stinson," I said.

"I didn't lose it, Mommy!" was Stinson's reply. "I gave it to Jesus!"

The person who is living a praying life learns that nothing you give to Jesus is lost. Giving the thing you love best to the One you love most is what brings exuberant joy, the hallmark of the praying life.

Do you have any "red balloons" you're clutching? Is there anything you need to give to Jesus—just because you love Him? Let go of what you're holding on to and experience His joy. Write your thoughts.

What you have to give up in order to reach your goal will feel more like being freed of weights. *"Let us throw off everything that hinders and the sin that so easily entangles, and let us run with perseverance the race marked out for us"* (Hebrews 12:1). What we once considered gain we now see as loss. What we once counted as treasure we now know is rubbish.

But whatever was to my profit I now consider loss for the sake of Christ. What is more, I consider everything a loss compared to the surpassing greatness of knowing Christ Jesus my Lord, for whose sake I have lost all things. I consider them rubbish, that I may gain Christ. —Philippians 3:7–8

The praying life is a life of diligence. In the praying life, we welcome Him as the Refiner's Fire, burning away every distraction. To the physical ears such a call sounds harsh and unappealing. To the ears of faith it is like a *"perfume poured out"* (Song of Songs 1:3). The heart of the seeker responds, *"Show me your face, let me hear your voice; for your voice is sweet, and your face is lovely"* (Song of Songs 2:14).

Week 13, Day 1

PRACTICE A NEW WAY OF PRAYING

Pray with Thomas à Kempis, "What Thou wilt; as Thou wilt; when Thou wilt."

_____

_____

_____

_____

_____

DAY TWO

A praying life cannot be scheduled. It has to flow. Yet specific times of uninterrupted prayer must be scheduled. Disciplined times of prayer merge into and become part of the praying life. Jesus gave guidance about structuring prayer times: *"When you pray, go into your room, close the door and pray to your Father, who is unseen. Then your Father, who sees what is done in secret, will reward you"* (Matthew 6:6). Let's closely examine what He says about scheduled prayer.

The Habit

"When you pray..." We must have the habit of praying. A habit is an action that has become fixed in one's life through repetition. The decision to perform a habit is settled. Every day I perform numerous tasks without stopping to decide whether or not I will perform them. They are habits. There are, for example, personal grooming actions I perform without giving them a second thought. Every day I check my email, go the post office, check my voice mail—all by habit.

What caused these actions to become habit? First, I am convinced of their importance. Second, I have fixed them in my life by repetition.

What defines them as habit? I do not struggle with a decision to perform these actions every day. The decision to perform them was made at some time in the past. I do them automatically. Not to do them would be unusual—I would have to make a decision not to do them.

Scheduled periods of prayer should become our habit. If we are convinced of the value of daily uninterrupted time with the Father, we should begin to fix that action in our lives through repetition.

Scheduled periods of prayer should become our habit. If we are convinced of the value of daily uninterrupted time with the Father, we should begin to fix that action in our lives through repetition.

What are some things that you do every day without daily deciding anew to do them?

What is it about each of these activities that causes you to have such a wholehearted commitment to them that you don't even consider not performing them?

Do you have that same wholehearted commitment to a daily time of prayer?

Write out what you know would be the benefits of a daily prayer time.

Are those benefits attractive enough to you to be worth the sacrifice?

The decision to rise early for extended times of prayer turns on a few seconds. The first seconds after the alarm clock rings decide your action. "*As a door turns on its hinges, so a sluggard turns on his bed*" (Proverbs 26:14). At the moment the alarm clock rings, choose—will you be sluggish or diligent? Will you choose sleep or prayer?

I went past the field of the sluggard, past the vineyard of the man who lacks judgment; thorns had come up everywhere, the ground was covered with weeds, and the stone wall was in ruins. I applied my heart to what I observed and learned a lesson from what I saw. —Proverbs 24:30–32

This is a description of the life of a sluggard. The prayer life, left unattended, is overgrown with weeds, broken down, in disrepair. A praying life requires diligence, or spiritual poverty will sneak up on you and overtake you. Be like the person in the proverb: Apply your heart to what you observe and learn a lesson from what you see.

In contrast to the life of a sluggard, God wants to make your life like a watered garden. He wants to tend, protect, and maintain it Himself. "*I, the LORD, watch over it; I water it continually. I guard it day and night so that no one may harm it*" (Isaiah 27:3).

When morning comes, don't choose "*a little sleep, a little slumber, a little folding of the hands to rest—and poverty will come on you like a bandit and scarcity like an armed man*" (Proverbs 24:33–34). The enemy is waiting to steal your spiritual health; inattention to a daily time of focused prayer will give him just the opportunity he seeks to leave you spiritually impoverished.

To fix a habit, experts give this advice:

1. Begin immediately.

2. Never allow an exception to occur.

3. Do not consider the action an option.

When your alarm clock goes off, keep moving. Don't allow yourself one minute or five minutes to decide whether or not you will get up for prayer. The decision is fixed, now fix the behavior. Within a few minutes of getting up, the difficulty is over. If your lifestyle, health, or schedule is such that early morning is not an option for scheduled prayer time, let God show you what time of the day you are to set aside for Him. Keep that appointment diligently.

Isaiah 50:4 says, "*He wakens me morning by morning, wakens my ear to listen like one being taught.*" Who will assign you the time you should be up for time with the Father?

Right now, ask the Father what time He wants you to set aside as time for Him alone. Write down what you sense Him saying.

Now, ask Him to wake you at that time. I find that I often wake up several minutes before my alarm clock is set to go off. Ask Him to awaken you with a sense of expectancy and to impart to you His own eagerness for time with you.

Week 13, Day 2

PRACTICE A NEW WAY OF PRAYING

Pray with Thomas à Kempis, "What Thou wilt; as Thou wilt; when Thou wilt."

_____

_____

_____

_____

_____

_____

DAY THREE

The Place

"*When you pray, go into your room, close the door…*" As part of establishing the habit of daily prayer, we should, as often as possible, use the same location. By choosing a designated location, you will have one less decision to make. You can have your Bible and prayer journal, or whatever materials you use, already in place. The more routine the outward behaviors are, the more energy is focused on the inward activities. When you don't have to give thought to the functional details, you will come to prayer less distracted, more ready to listen to Him.

When you enter into your room, you are to shut the door. You need to choose a place where life's distractions will be less likely to infringe. Your location should not become so important, though, that you feel you can miss your prayer time if your location is not available. Your true inner room is within you.

What is a convenient place for you to engage in daily extended prayer time? What do you need to do to make it inviting?

The Focus

"When you pray… pray to your Father, who is unseen." The purpose of your prayer time is to give God your undivided attention. It is not for the purpose of securing His favor for the day. His favor rests on you forever. A morning prayer time should not be viewed superstitiously. Sometimes I hear people say something like, "When I have a prayer time, my day goes well. When I skip it, I have a bad day." Morning prayer is not a magic powder to sprinkle on your day. If you have a habit of morning prayer, it will be followed by some good days and some bad days. The difference will be that you will be centered in God and will react differently to both good and bad.

The focus of your prayer time is God Himself. This is not your one chance to get His attention. You will be walking in prayer all day and all night. You don't have to feel compelled to get all your prayer requests in at this time, as if this will be your only chance. The agenda for your morning prayer time is to hear God, to reaffirm His rule in your life. *"He wakens me morning by morning, wakens my ear to listen like one being taught"* (Isaiah 50:4). This verse causes me to picture a disciple sitting at his teacher's feet, leaning forward so as not to miss one word that falls from the master's lips. In your time of prayer, listen like one being taught.

What is the focus of your times of prayer—the Father or your own agenda? Will you commit to refocus your prayer times?

The Response

"Your Father, who sees what is done in secret, will reward you." Jesus said that those who pray so that others will admire them will have the reward they seek. Their spiritual lives may well be applauded and admired. However, they will have settled for a cheap reward. They will not be rewarded with the presence of God. Theirs will be a perishable crown.

The reward God offers is Himself; and that will be more than enough. In His presence we find everything we are looking for. He is our very great reward.

Have you come to the place in your praying life that God Himself is all you truly desire? Is everything else optional? If not, ask Him to bring your life to that point.

Week 13, Day 3

PRACTICE A NEW WAY OF PRAYING
Pray with Thomas à Kempis, "What Thou wilt; as Thou wilt; when Thou wilt."

_____

_____

_____

_____

_____

_____

DAY FOUR

Prayer takes many forms. A single "right" formula for prayer does not exist. However, it can be helpful to have an outline to structure extended times of prayer. A structure can help you keep your thoughts focused. My challenge to you is to spend a full hour every day in uninterrupted prayer.

An outline can keep you from feeling overwhelmed at the thought of an hour in prayer.

"*And when you pray, do not keep on babbling like pagans, for they think they will be heard because of their many words*" (Matthew 6:7). The secret to an hour in prayer is not an hour filled with your words. An avalanche of words will not move God. It is not the cry of the lips, but the cry of the heart that God hears.

Many people are intimidated by the thought of praying for extended periods of time. "I can't imagine praying for an hour. What would I say?" We don't need to come to God with an approach mapped out. Not knowing what to say will relieve the pray-er of one barrier to true prayer: a predetermined agenda. We don't need to come to Him with a planned speech. Come to listen first, speak second. Remember Habakkuk? "*I will stand at my watch and station myself on the ramparts; I will look to see what he will say to me, and what answer I am to give to this complaint*" (Habakkuk 2:1). Prayer is really answering God. It is responding to His voice, to His initiative. Let Him stir up prayer in you. The key to extended times of prayer is not much speaking, but much listening.

Let Him stir up prayer in you. The key to extended times of prayer is not much speaking, but much listening.

Jesus gave a simple outline for extended prayer times. In this outline, He showed us the many forms prayer will take. Many have found that using this as a basic structure, a pray-er can keep his mind on track. However, please keep in mind that this is only a structure; it is not a rule. Let the Holy Spirit fill the structure however He wants to.

"This, then, is how you should pray: Our Father in heaven, hallowed be your name, your kingdom come, your will be done on earth as it is in heaven. Give us today our daily bread. Forgive us our debts, as we also have forgiven our debtors. And lead us not into temptation, but deliver us from the evil one." —Matthew 6:9–13

❖

Take the Lord's Prayer apart phrase by phrase and list the forms and aspects of prayer Jesus mentioned.

Our Father in heaven, hallowed be your name,

Your kingdom come, your will be done on earth as it is in heaven.

Give us today our daily bread.

Forgive us our debts, as we also have forgiven our debtors.

And lead us not into temptation, but deliver us from the evil one.

Praising the Father

Let's examine the different forms of prayer listed in Jesus' outline. Why is it helpful to begin focused prayer times with praise? By beginning times of prayer with praise, we immediately put the spotlight in the right place. The focus of our prayer times is to be God. As we spend time considering Him, reflecting on His greatness, we build a foothold for our faith. Against the backdrop of His majesty, life takes on its proper perspective.

Authentically and genuinely praising God moves you into a position of faith, from which anything can be accomplished. *"Everything is possible for him who believes,"* Jesus told us in Mark 9:23. Anything is possible! The praying person who takes the time to consider the works and the attributes of God will be filled with faith.

The praying person who takes the time to consider and recognize that the very One who performed all the recorded miracles, signs and wonders in the Scripture is his or her "Abba"—Daddy—will be unable not to believe. For that person, unbelief would be the most unnatural state imaginable. He is our Father. Yet He is clothed with splendor and majesty. He is covered with light as with a cloak. He commands the morning and causes the dawn to know its place. He is great in wisdom and mighty in deed. For Him, all the morning stars sang together and all the sons of God shouted for joy. The idols tremble at His presence and the hearts of His enemies melt within them. Great is the Lord. He is greatly to be praised. And He is your Father, who watches over you obsessively and lavishes love on you.

My earthly father recently retired from a career that included being an attorney, a legislator, a circuit judge, and finally a judge on the Missouri Court of Appeals. During his retirement festivities, people who had known him in various roles praised him. Some praised him for being a defender and protector, others praised him as a worthy adversary, still others said that he was a fair and balanced creator of law, while others had known him as a wise dispenser of justice and interpreter of law. All of the praise was true and justified. But it fell short of the full picture of who my father is. His admirers missed the big picture because he's not their daddy.

I know someone entirely different because I know him as "Daddy." As my daddy, I've known him as protector and defender; as my daddy, I've known him as a dispenser of justice and a creator of law. But do you see the difference it makes to know him in these roles as my daddy? When those roles are being enacted with personal, directed love as their motivating force, they have a different effect altogether.

Consider who God is. Consider His power, strength, and wisdom. Then realize that all He is and all He does flows out to you from a core of personal, intimate love. He is your Daddy. If *daddy* is not a word that brings up good feelings, realize that God is the kind of daddy you long to have.

Praise the LORD, O my soul; all my inmost being, praise his holy name. Praise the LORD, O my soul, and forget not all his benefits. —Psalm 103:1–2

Stop now and praise the Father, using Psalm 96 to shape your prayers. Keep in mind as you are focusing on His power that He is your Father. Read through the psalm, stopping to absorb and respond to each thought. Turn it into a celebration of praise.

Interceding

Jesus, in His outline, leads us next to intercession: directing the will and the power of God into situations on earth. "Let Your kingdom come. Let Your will be done on earth like Your will is done in heaven." Exodus 28:29–30 gives a wonderful picture of intercession.

"Whenever Aaron enters the Holy Place, he will bear the names of the sons of Israel over his heart on the breastpiece of decision as a continuing memorial before the LORD. Also put the Urim and the Thummim in the breastpiece, so they may be over Aaron's heart whenever he enters the presence of the LORD. Thus Aaron will always bear the means of making decisions for the Israelites over his heart before the LORD." —Exodus 28:29–30

In intercession, we carry those in need over our hearts before the Lord continually. God will engrave the names of those for whom we are to diligently intercede on our hearts. We must allow God to give us intercession assignments. We cannot be an earnest intercessor for every need. God will place some needs on your heart and you will feel the burden of intercession for them. Other needs you will not.

When God assigns you responsibility for prolonged intercession in regard to some need, you are to bear it on your heart before Him. Sometimes, however, He just brings you into an ongoing intercession for a moment. When someone brings you a need, immediately—even as they are telling you about it—lift it to the Father. If He intends to burden you with it for intense intercession, you will know. Otherwise, any time it comes to your mind, pray a "flash prayer." Frank Laubach introduces the idea of "flash prayers" in his book, *Prayer: The Mightiest Force in the World.* "Everybody in every ordinary day has hundreds of chinks of idle wasted time which may be filled with *flash prayers* ten seconds or a minute long." I have a bulletin board in my office that I think of as my flash prayer board. I keep on it pictures or other reminders and as my eye falls on them during the day, I flash a prayer. Also, every time I see a person who has asked me for prayer or who has a need I know about, I flash a prayer. Or when a person comes to my mind, I flash a prayer. Usually, the content of my flash prayer is nothing but the name of Jesus.

Some needs, however, will jump into your heart and make themselves at home. The Spirit of prayer will call upon you to persevere in prayer for these needs until He takes away the burden. Frank Laubach explains what happens when we pray for others: "A mighty invisible spiritual force lifts our minds and eyes toward God. His Spirit flows through our prayer to them, and He can speak to them directly." The heart of intercession is "Your kingdom come, Your will be done on earth as it is in heaven."

What are the needs that God has engraved on your heart to bear before Him continually? Spend some time letting the Spirit flow through your prayers to the people involved.

Spend some time letting your mind, guided by His Spirit, practice "flash prayers."

Week 13, Day 4

PRACTICE A NEW WAY OF PRAYING
Pray with Thomas à Kempis, "What Thou wilt; as Thou wilt; when Thou wilt."

_____

_____

_____

_____

DAY FIVE

Petition for Daily Needs

The next phrase in Jesus' prayer outline is, "*Give us this day our daily bread.*" He tells us to come to our Father with our daily material needs. He tells us not to be anxious about our physical needs because our Father knows about them and cares about them (Matthew 6:25–34). We are not to be anxious, but instead to ask God to provide for our daily needs.

God is practical. He created and ordered the universe. He knows and cares about your material needs. After all, He created you with needs. He could have created us so that we had no material needs; so that we were self-sufficient. But He chose to create our physical structures so that they need food and shelter. He wants us to come to Him for our daily supply so that we will learn to trust Him. Our needs are His entry points.

What are your needs today? Ask the Father to supply them.

Forgiven and Forgiving

Next in the outline is "*Forgive us our debts, as we forgive our debtors.*" Incorporate into your prayer time an opportunity for God to bring to your attention anything that is cluttering your heart and making your life unavailable to Him.

As we approach God in confession, it is a time for Him to shine His holy light on our hearts and lives, examining both motives and actions.

Confession is not to be an exercise in self-loathing. It is a time to let God search our hearts. It is not our duty to find our faults and tell God about them; it is His place to show us the dark corners. Our part is to confess and forsake what God shows us. We need to open our lives to Him so He can bring conviction.

Search me, O God, and know my heart; test me and know my anxious thoughts. See if there is any offensive way in me, and lead me in the way everlasting. —Psalm 139:23–24

When we feel that we are to dredge up our faults for confession, we are focused in the wrong place. We are looking at ourselves when we should be looking at God. Several things can happen.

1. **We may become so discouraged that we feel unworthy of God's love.** One of Satan's most effective ploys is to accuse and condemn. He loves to load us down with a sense of failure and hopelessness. The Holy Spirit's conviction is different from the enemy's condemnation.
2. **We may become proud of how humble we are.**
3. **We may mask the true sin by concentrating on a symptom.** We may repent of an action, when it is an underlying attitude that needs cleansing.

The Holy Spirit will bring what was hidden into the light. Our part is to agree with Him and confess our sins. His part is to forgive our sins and cleanse us from all unrighteousness.

Specifically, the Spirit will be bringing to your attention anyone whom you need to forgive. If we are walking in the light—keeping nothing in the dark—then we are living in fellowship with other believers. This requires a consistent exchange of mercy and forgiveness between and among believers. "*If we walk in the light, as he is in the light, we have fellowship with one another*" (1 John 1:7).

Open your life to God's conviction. What is He telling you is cluttering your life?

Spiritual Warfare

Jesus brings His prayer outline to a close with these words: *"And lead us not into temptation, but deliver us from the evil one"* (Matthew 6:13). All prayer is spiritual warfare. Every prayer that gains ground for God's kingdom loses ground for the enemy. To pray is to be locked in combat with spiritual forces. Spiritual warfare is not a single type of praying; prayer is warfare. There is no reason for this to be an intimidating thought. The two opposing sides in this warfare are not equal. Satan's army is pitifully weak and small compared to God's.

"The one who is in you is greater than the one who is in the world."
—1 John 4:4

"Don't be afraid," the prophet answered. "Those who are with us are more than those who are with them.' And Elisha prayed, 'O LORD, open his eyes so he may see." Then the LORD opened the servant's eyes, and he looked and saw the hills full of horses and chariots of fire all around Elisha.
—2 Kings 6:16–17

Satan is a defeated foe. His forces are already defeated. They were defeated at the Cross. *"Having disarmed the powers and authorities, he made a public spectacle of them, triumphing over them by the cross"* (Colossians 2:15).

Satan's only weapon against the intercessor is propaganda. He wages an ingenious propaganda campaign tailor-made for each individual intercessor in order to keep us from invading and driving him out of territory he is occupying. Whatever propaganda he uses against you, it is meant to keep you from invading and persevering until the battle is finished. If you enter the battle, you will find Satan and his forces defenseless against you. There may be skirmishes and pockets of resistance, but the outcome is not in question. You are protected by full body armor and His name is Jesus. *"Your life is now hidden with Christ in God"* (Colossians 3:3). *"For all of you who were baptized into Christ have clothed yourselves with Christ"* (Galatians 3:27). He is your spiritual armor. No weapon formed against you can prosper.

A new kind of weapon that has been used in warfare recently is the "smart bomb." These are computer-driven bombs that hit a precise target. These bombs don't land in the general area of the target, they actually go through a window or down an elevator shaft. They are exact.

As Satan has occupied territory, he has built strongholds, or fortresses. He has built these fortresses out of arguments and pretensions that set themselves up against the knowledge of God. Think of your Spirit-directed prayers as "smart bombs" landing on enemy strongholds. Your persevering prayers are precisely and systematically destroying Satan's hold.

Satan's lies are protected by a fortress built of pretensions that set themselves up against the knowledge of God. His strongholds preserve his lies by keeping them from being exposed to the truth.

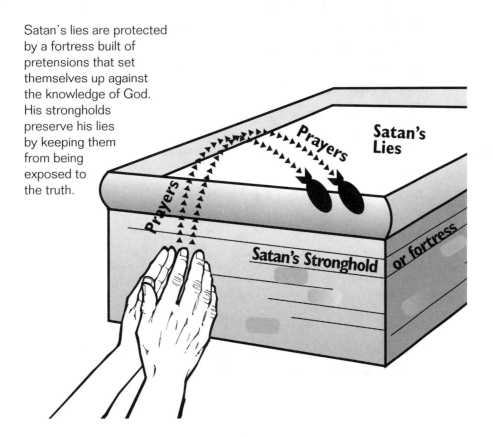

Jesus' prayer outline teaches us to ask for deliverance from the evil one—rescue us from the lies and distortions of the evil one. Satan's tactics are called wily schemes. "*In order that Satan might not outwit us. For we are not unaware of his schemes*" (2 Corinthians 2:11). We should "*put on the full armor of God so that you can take your stand against the devil's schemes*" (Ephesians 6:11).

The word translated "schemes" is the Greek word *naoma*, which means "a carefully thought-out plan; a purposeful thought." Satan has a plan and he is working toward a goal. He carries out his plan with lies, distortions, and disguises. He is depicted as a master of disguises, wrapping himself in robes of light. He is also a master of propaganda meant to break your morale and dilute your resolve. To counter his schemes, we must be well acquainted with the truth. His approach from the beginning has been to distort the truth and make his lies seem perfectly reasonable. It is by living a praying life that the enemy's schemes will be exposed and we will be delivered from his lies.

❖

Which of these propaganda campaigns does Satan use against you?

• *You're not good enough. What makes you think God would listen to you?*
• *Prayer has never worked for you before. What makes you think it will work this time?*
• *You're so busy right now. Pray later. Tomorrow, start having a disciplined prayertime.*
• *If you really get involved in prayer, Satan will cause terrible things to happen in your life.*
• Other:

What is the truth? Write it out.

Reflect on what the Spirit of prayer has taught you through these 13 weeks of study. In your own words, what is a praying life?

State what you believe to be the most life-changing concept you encountered in your study.

What commitments are you willing to make to have a praying life?

Week 13, Day 5

<u>PRACTICE A NEW WAY OF PRAYING</u>

Pray with Thomas à Kempis, "What Thou wilt; as Thou wilt; when Thou wilt."

_____

_____

_____

_____

Week Thirteen Anniversary Thought

Giving God the firstfruits of your day will set the course of your focus. Many people find the daily discipline of prayer the biggest challenge. Let me make a few suggestions.

- Pray actively. Walk through your house and pray in each room, or walk through your neighborhood and pray as you go.

- Set up the space where you will have your time with the Lord before you go to bed. Set it up so that it is inviting and appealing to you. Have your Bible and your prayer journal, worship music, candles, coffee ready to go … whatever sets the stage for an intimate encounter. Make it a ceremony.

- Put your alarm clock across the room from your bed so you have to jump out of bed to turn it off.

- When you sit up on the side of your bed, instead of *flopping back down and* pulling the covers back over your head, consider it your morning offering to the Lord.

- If you get out of the habit, shake it off and start again.

Find ways that work for you to keep the discipline of daily time devoted to the Lord's voice.

The Fruit of Suffering

Over the years that the message of this book grew in me, honed in the trenches of daily living, I had my husband at my side, cheering me on, shouldering the burdens and sharing the joys. Fellow-learner, sounding board, advisor, protector. Wayne is no longer at my side. He passed away in 2005. He lived a praying life, and when the end of his time on earth came, he met it with astonishing courage and peace. I kept a blog during his illness so that people could stay informed. As I would add an entry, usually more bad news, he would always say, "But tell them it is well with my soul."

We learned much from how he lived, but we learned even more from how he died. Does a praying life work, even when your world is coming apart at the seams? It does. The principles can stand the most arduous test and prove true.

Wayne and I were partners both in life and in ministry. Wayne was a businessman and had spent his business career with large corporations. Though he was successful in all the measurable ways, he always felt a great discontent that what he accomplished every day had no eternal value. He understood that the lives he touched along the way were the real reason for his employment, but he had a restlessness that I think was always a call to ministry. In the very early years of my ministry, he was my biggest cheerleader. When I was tempted to sit back and let opportunities pass by, he was the one who prodded me forward. He was always willing to take on the extra work that fell to him while I met deadlines and traveled to speak. He didn't think of it as a burden, since it just meant taking care of our three young sons—his favorite thing to do.

At a certain point when the ministry seemed to be ready to take a big step forward, but to take it would mean much pressure on the family, Wayne decided to take a huge leap of faith and leave his secular career to be a full-time manager and president of our ministry. He put all his skills and his experience and his relational skills to work running the Praying Life Foundation. No paycheck. No company car. No company trips. Just three little boys and a wife he believed in.

I tell you this to say that this ministry of mine is ours. We grew it from a corner of our dining room to a full-time ministry with office and employees and volunteers. Side by side. Praying together through every decision, every opportunity, every redirection along the way. Even when, in his last years, he went back to a full-time job in a ministry area he loved, he still was fully involved in everything about the Praying Life Foundation.

In October of 2005, thinking we were finally about to get an answer for the dizziness that had been diagnosed as an inner ear infection, instead we got the dreadful news that Wayne had an advanced case of an aggressive brain cancer, for which there was essentially no hope of cure. Two months later, he went to be with the Lord. December 13. Two weeks before Christmas.

When the fog lifted, and I began to realize that I was a WIDOW, of all things—I could not imagine continuing in the ministry that had always been us, never just me. The thought of taking on a new project or coming up with a fresh thought seemed impossible. I couldn't say a whole sentence without breaking into sobs.

The first year of my widowhood was excruciating. Unless I was speaking—where a mantle of strength would simply fall on me—I couldn't leave my house because I never knew what memory might ambush me and send me into a tailspin right in public. I started explaining to my friends and my sons, "A widow lives in my body and I don't know her. I don't know how she'll act. I don't know what to expect from her. I can't let her out in public." The end of the first year, Christmas came again. All my sons came home. We prepared to attend Christmas Eve services, one of my husband's favorite things, and I had to gather myself up emotionally. My sons—who were not used to having a mom who cried all the time—hovered around me and kept asking me, "Are you OK, Mom?" And it hit me: Oh my goodness! I'm fragile!

I had never been fragile before. It woke me up. I'm not supposed to be fragile. I had taught for years about embracing the pain of crucifixion because it is the only path to resurrection. Did I mean to add, "Except if your husband dies unexpectedly"? Something snapped inside. Wayne faced his death with courage and dignity. Surely I could do as much.

I realize that the great wound inflicted on my heart has made me desperately dependent on God in a way I never would have known otherwise. I know a level of supernatural comfort from the Father that can't be explained. It has to be experienced. I know something I can't say in words, but that has transformed my ministry and given it a new depth. I can see so many provisions along the way that I didn't recognize at the time.

For example, when my husband decided to be my full-time manager, from then on we worked together every day. My sons, who would lose their father early, had more of his presence than most sons have in a long lifetime. It reminds me that God is always thinking ahead. Nothing is spontaneous or comes to my life without a solid foundation laid. I never need to say, "Oh, God! Do something!" Just, "Oh, God! What have you already done and how can I position myself to be in the flow of Your provision?"

I am just through my third year of widowhood. I feel like myself again. The widow and I have integrated. I'm not fragile anymore, but now I can be patient with others who are fragile.

I think it is easier to tell people that we can avoid suffering and be protected from all pain than it is to tell people that pain is unavoidable and is to be embraced for the work it will do in our lives. We have this mentality that says that every bad thing that happens is Satan attacking. Maybe it is God pruning. Isn't it interesting that the branch bearing much fruit gets not protected, not babied, not put in a dust-proof display cabinet for all to admire, but pruned. Cut back. Injured. And why? So that it can bear more fruit.

If we cherish our comfort and value our status quo, then we can never let pain in to do its transforming work. If we resent the intrusion of crucifixion, then we will never experience the wonder of resurrection.

Those we lead and influence suffer. They have suffered, they will suffer, they are suffering. Unless we can display our wounds, others can't see the power of pain.

Years before this experience, I wrote these words in my book *He Restores My Soul*:

The body of His resurrection was perfect and eternal. It is the very body in which He ascended from earth to take His place at the right hand of the Father. This perfect, resurrected body retained its scars.

How often our pride, or our mistaken sense that we need to present a perfect front to those in our care, causes us to think of our wounds and our scars as something to hide; something ugly; something demeaning; something that lessens our value. But look at Jesus. Look at what Jesus thought of His wounds: "Here, Thomas. Look at My wounds. Touch My scars. These are the proof of My resurrection. I bear the marks of death, but I am alive!" Jesus knew His wounds were beautiful.... At the places where I am broken, the power of Christ is authenticated in me for others. Where I have submitted to the crucifixion, the power of the resurrection is put on display. I can say, "Look at my wounds. Touch my scars. I have death-wounds, but I am alive." I can wear my wounds without shame. They tell a resurrection story.

I have to remember to let my strength come out of weakness. Those moments when I am overwhelmed with loss and aware that decisions are mine alone to make become moments when I am brought back to the all-sufficient Jesus, who is the storehouse of all wisdom and knowledge. I have to trust that the work of my woundedness is showing up in ministry, though it can't be pinpointed or identified on a chart. I have to let my wounds show, so they can bring hope to those whom God has entrusted to me.

Contrary to one of our much quoted bromides, God *will* give you more than you can bear. *"We were under great pressure, far beyond our ability to endure, so that we despaired even of life. Indeed, in our hearts we felt the sentence of death. But this happened that we might not rely on ourselves but on God, who raises the dead"* (2 Corinthians 1:8–9). God is not the great burden-giver, testing you to see just how much He can pile on you and still leave you standing. He is the burden-bearer. When we learn to hand over burdens in the daily issues of life, we'll be ready when the big ones come along.

At some point in the very depths of my grief, I asked the Lord, "If You bear my burdens, then why do I have to feel this pain?" I thought about an experience when my son Kennedy asked me to put my hands against his punching bag and hold it steady for him to punch. Big, strong, Kennedy put all his power into the punch. On my side, it stung my hands just enough for me to say, "Ouch!" But it was nothing like the pain that I would have experienced had the punch landed on me. I'd have been knocked out!

The Lord seemed to say to me: I stand between you and any blows headed your way. The blows meant for you land on Me. If the pain you feel hurts, just imagine the blow I absorbed for you. It should have been a knockout punch, but you will never feel the full force of a blow.

A praying life—a life lived in the flow of His power and provision—does not promise life without pain. It promises life without knockout punches.

A praying life—a life lived in the flow of His power and provision—does not promise life without pain. It promises life without knockout punches.

PS *Early in his illness, Wayne and I had time to muse on what the experience of dying might be like. We agreed it must be like a birth. Imagine a little baby in the womb. It's the only world he knows. His universe is small and dark, but he doesn't know that. Those of us out here in the big world think,* How crowded you must be. Why, your world can barely hold you! Every move you make leads you to boundaries. I'm sure you must be eager to come out into light and air. *But the little baby—he thinks he is in light and air. How amazed he must be when he pushes through the birth canal and encounters the big world.*

Here on earth, we think we know light and air, but we only know the outside edges, a little caricature. How amazed we will be when we push through that eternal birth canal and find Life.

December 13, 2005. Wayne Dean was born.

One. Jennifer's Recommended Reading List

When I first began my spiritual search in earnest, my dad gave me a book titled *Prayer* by Ole Hallesby. Over the years, he bought this book in bulk and gave away hundreds. This book addressed the questions I had about prayer. No formulas, no recipes, just relationship. It laid the groundwork for everything else I would piece together about prayer. Here I first learned that prayer begins with God, who puts the desires of His heart on mine.

With this foundational understanding in place, all the other pieces began to fall into place. I devoured books by other authors of that period (generally, the late nineteenth century through the early twentieth century). I cut my teeth on their rich works. They trained me to see the Scripture through a new prism. They didn't tell stories, they expounded the Scripture. When I finished one of their books, I didn't know much more about them, but I knew much more about God. To this day, I could not tell you much about the people whose work helped shape me so significantly. I'm going to list for you a sampling of books by my favorite authors.

Prayer by Ole Hallesby

With Christ in the School of Prayer by Andrew Murray

The True Vine by Andrew Murray

Abundant Living by E. Stanley Jones

Mastery: The Art of Mastering Life by E. Stanley Jones

Christian Disciplines by Oswald Chambers

A Testament of Devotion by Thomas R. Kelly

Experiencing the Depths of Jesus Christ by Jeanne Guyon

The Dynamic of All-Prayer by G. Granger Fleming

How to Pray by R. A. Torrey

Letters to Malcolm by C. S. Lewis

Mere Christianity by C. S. Lewis

Prayer, The Mightiest Force in the World by Frank C. Laubach

The Life of Abraham by F. B. Meyer

The Way Into the Holiest by F. B. Meyer

The Saving Life of Christ by W. Ian Thomas

Quiet Talks on Prayer by S. D. Gordon

Two. Man's Will/God's Sovereignty

In the Scripture, the doctrines of man's will and God's sovereignty are both evident. For example, Jesus says, *"whoever comes to me I will never drive away"* (John 6:37), which seems to suggest that man's free choice is the determinate force. However, the phrase that introduces this statement says, *"All that the Father gives me will come to me,"* which seems to suggest that God determines who will and will not come to Jesus. Together the statement reads, *"All that the Father gives me will come to me, and whoever comes to me I will never drive away."* Not just in the matter of salvation, but in the whole of life, these two truths are juxtaposed and can appear at a glance to be contradictory. Any doctrinal stance that teaches one and excludes the other is ignoring a fundamental teaching of the Word. Both have to be true if His Word is Truth (John 17:17).

It would certainly be naive of me to imagine that in a few paragraphs I can definitively put an end to the confusion. My purpose is to share with you what makes sense to me and what seems to me to be in accordance with *"the whole counsel of God"* (Acts 20:27 NKJV). Perhaps as you search the Scriptures and seek the Father, you will find these thoughts helpful.

Every argument must have a starting place—a central point. Here is mine: The Scripture is entirely true; it is true at every point; it is fully true. Therefore it contains no contradictions. If two truths fully taught in Scripture appear to contradict one another, then I am missing the understanding or knowledge that will logically and authentically bring the two truths together into one whole. This cannot be accomplished by contriving arguments or imposing meanings that will force truth into a palatable form. In other words, we can't make things up or add our own spin to make the Scripture say what we think it should. All truth is contained in the Word of God. The Scripture is its own commentary. The Spirit of God will lead you into all truth. He will disclose to you the *"riches stored in secret places"* (Isaiah 45:3). He will help you see the fullness of truth.

So there are no contradictions in Scripture because Scripture is truth. What is a contradiction? A contradiction is two things that cannot be true at the same time. The classic illustration of a contradiction is an immovable object and an irresistible force. If an immovable object and an irresistible force come together, one will be proven false. If the object moves in response to the force, the object is not immovable. If the object does not move in response to the force, the force is not irresistible. An immovable object and an irresistible force are a contradiction. If two things cannot be true at the same time, then one or the other is not fully true. In order to preserve my starting point—the Scripture is fully true and contains no contradictions—man's will and God's sovereignty must be fully true at the same time.

Now, let's put another piece into the puzzle. Let's add God's total foreknowledge. He foreknows every choice any human being will ever make. He does not coerce the choices, but He knows them. Add now a third element: God's all-powerfulness. He has all power. The earth and everything on it is subject to Him and He can prevent or allow anything.

Suppose that God foreknows a choice made out of a heart full of evil. Do you believe that God has the power to stop the acting out of that choice? I believe He does. It seems especially clear to me in the account of Jesus' earthly ministry, toward His last days on earth. His enemies many times sought to harm Him physically, but God did not allow it because the time was not ripe. Only when God's sovereign plan ordained that the moment had arrived for the arrest and crucifixion could Jesus' enemies put their hands on Him. They were making free will choices for evil intentions, yet God's sovereignty was fully in effect. *"This man was handed over to you by God's set purpose and foreknowledge; and you, with the help of wicked men, put him to death by nailing him to the cross"* (Acts 2:23). Below are several paragraphs about this from my book *Riches Stored In Secret Places.*

"Many are the plans in a man's heart, but it is the LORD's purpose that prevails" **(Proverbs 19:21). Man's thoughts and intentions are not hidden from God's view.** *"Nothing in all creation is hidden from God's sight. Everything is uncovered and laid bare before the eyes of him to whom we must give account"* **(Hebrews 4:13). The plans in a person's innermost being, even before those thoughts are fully formed, are known by God. Before a thought has fully evolved into a conscious thought—before it has taken the form of words—God knows it thoroughly.** *"Before a word is on my tongue you know it completely, O LORD"* **(Psalm 139:4). God knows the thoughts of all people, even those who are hostile to Him.** *"[Jesus] did not need man's testimony about man, for he knew what was in a man"* **(John 2:25). He is able to use even the thoughts and plans in the heart of a person—both believers and unbelievers—to bring about His divine purposes.**

Have you ever thought about how detailed and exactly timed the arrest, trial, crucifixion, burial, and resurrection of Jesus was? The exact timing had been established before the world began. God gave an elaborate and explicit picture of the timing when He established the feasts in the Old Covenant, generations before the event occurred in

history. Jesus had to be on the cross and dead by sundown on Passover because He is the Paschal Lamb. The exact incident had to occur by twilight on the fourteenth day of the first month, the month of Nisan. He had to be in the ground before 6 P.M. because He is the whole burnt offering sacrifice for the nation. He had to be in the ground three days and three nights because He was prophesied to be by Jonah in the belly of the whale. He had to be resurrected on the third day, the day following the Sabbath, the Feast of Firstfruits, because He is the Firstfruits of the Spirit. He had to be resurrected after sunset and before sunrise. Every detail of His ordeal was laid out in the beginning. God's timetable was exact. He did not deviate from it at all.

However, look at the events that put everything on this timetable. *"Now the Feast of Unleavened Bread, called the Passover, was approaching, and the chief priests and the teachers of the law were looking for some way to get rid of Jesus, for they were afraid of the people"* (Luke 22:1–2). At exactly the right moment, Jesus' enemies began to act on their festering hatred and fear of Him. Until that moment, Jesus had always said, *"My time is not yet come."* Until that time, His enemies' schemes could not succeed.

Because of their impatience to finish the deed before the Sabbath, Jesus' enemies called an unusual meeting of the Sanhedrin, then they woke Pilate, then Herod (who just happened to be in Jerusalem at that time), and finally Pilate again. What should have taken several days at least was railroaded through by enemies of God. Because of their manipulation of events, every event occurred exactly on God's predetermined timetable, the timetable He had planned from the beginning of time and announced early in Israel's history.

"The LORD works out everything for his own ends—even the wicked for a day of disaster" (Proverbs 16:4). Even Satan is nothing more than a pawn in God's hands. Observe Satan's part in God's plan: Between the temptation of Jesus and His crucifixion, Satan was watching for a perfect time to carry out his own agenda. *"When the devil had finished all this tempting, he left him until an opportune time"* (Luke 4:13). Now—at this exact moment—Satan sees his opportune time. *"Satan entered Judas.... And Judas went to the chief priests and the officers of the temple guard and discussed with them how he might betray Jesus.... He...watched for an opportunity to hand Jesus over to them when no crowd was present"* (Luke 22:3–6). Satan had found the opportune time for which he had been watching. The irony is that it was God's opportune time, not Satan's.

Through every page of Scripture God shows us His ways. He uses everything to work out His own purposes. His purpose will prevail no matter what plans are in the hearts of men. Every one of God's enemies, though they plotted and fought against His people, became the means to His end. You and I, His children who are in covenant relationship with Him, are never at the mercy of any person or any circumstance. God is never taken by surprise at any person's decisions or actions. He has already factored them in to His purpose and plan for us.

Rest in the fact that God is managing every detail in order to work out His purposes. *"All the ways of the Lord are loving and faithful"* (Psalm 25:10). Nothing is left to chance.

If God foreknows evil choices and has the power to stop them but instead allows them, then you can be assured that even this evil is moving events toward the end God has in mind.

These few inadequate words do not begin to address the many questions these two mighty doctrines give birth to. But maybe they will give you a few anchoring thoughts to begin or continue your own inquiry of the Lord. Remember that the Father invites you to come to Him so that He can reason with you; He invites you to set your arguments before Him so that He can show you truth.

Don't let God's foreknowledge and sovereignty take on an out-of-balance place in your thinking. You are dealing with God, and God with you, in the now. C. S. Lewis wrote this in a letter to a friend:

Don't bother about the idea that "God has known for millions of years what you are about to pray." God is hearing you now, just as simply as a mother hears a child. The difference His timelessness makes is that this now (which slips away from you even as you say the word now) is for Him infinite. —C. S. Lewis, *Letters* (1 August 1949)

A detailed, careful look at this subject from Scripture is available in a paper titled: "Sovereign: When the Sovereignty of God and the Will of Man Intersect" by Jennifer Kennedy Dean. You may obtain the paper by:

1. Downloading it from www.prayinglife.org (find it under FAQ).
2. Calling our order line 1-888-844-6647 to request a copy.
3. Sending an email to resources@prayinglife.org to request the paper in an attached file.

Three. Is God's Sovereignty Limited to Man's Obedience?

Suppose Moses had ignored God's call to stand in the gap (see Ezekiel 22). Would God's will have been thwarted? Did the fulfillment of God's plan rest with Moses? If God was willing to save Judah, but didn't because there was no one to intercede, wasn't God's sovereignty limited by man's disobedience?

If so, then God's power is hostage to man's choices. Is that the God of the Bible? Does the fulfillment of God's plan depend on how man acts? If so, then how could God state with certainty what will happen in times to come?

God foreknows all choices. Nothing takes Him by surprise. He is not working contingently. God is not saying, "If Joe makes choice A, I'll do this. But if Joe makes choice B, I'll do something else. I'll have to wait and see what Joe chooses." God knows what choice Joe will make and His plan already takes it into consideration. He is sovereign over the end, but He is also sovereign over the means. He knew that at the right moment Moses would be available to intercede, opening the way for God to do what He had planned. In the case of Judah, God knew that there would be no intercessor, and Judah's captivity was factored into God's long-term plan. In these instances, God gives us a glimpse of the big picture so we can see what prayer accomplishes. He is saying, "This is what prayer held back; this is what lack of prayer produced."

In the covenant under which we live, the New Covenant, the Holy Spirit indwells each believer; God always has an intercessor. *"Because you are sons, God sent the Spirit of his Son into our hearts, the Spirit who calls out, 'Abba, Father'"* (Galatians 4:6). We live in a perfect and eternal covenant (Hebrews 13:20). In other words, it has no loopholes. Christ is fully present in the church; His fullness dwells in the church. (See Ephesians 1:22–23.) God has set up the cosmos to work in this way: The conduit that brings His will to earth is prayer. He has not set up a system that limits Him. God has an army of men and women who are keeping their lives available to Him so that the Spirit of prayer can pray through them. These intercessors may not know the details of what they are praying for, but the Spirit is always translating their words into the perfect will of God as they pray. *"In the same way, the Spirit helps us in our weakness. We do not know what we ought to pray for, but the Spirit himself intercedes for us with groans that words cannot express"* (Romans 8:26).

O Lord, you are my God; I will exalt you and praise your name, for in perfect faithfulness you have done marvelous things, things planned long ago.
—Isaiah 25:1

"Have you not heard? Long ago I ordained it. In days of old I planned it; now I have brought it to pass." —Isaiah 37:26

Four. Does God Change His Mind?

Several events recorded in the Old Testament might leave you with the idea that God changed His mind. A surface reading would suggest just that, but digging deeper and reading within the context of all of Scripture will give you a different viewpoint.

One of the events that people often point to as evidence that God's mind can be changed is found in Genesis 18:16–33, when Abraham and God discussed the destruction of Sodom and Gomorrah. The account begins like this: *"Then the LORD said, 'Shall I hide from Abraham what I am about to do? Abraham will surely become a great and powerful nation, and all nations on earth will be blessed through him. For I have chosen him, so that he will direct his children and his household after him to keep the way of the LORD by doing what is right and just, so that the LORD will bring about for Abraham what he has promised him.'"* (Genesis 18:17–19).

The Lord puts His thoughts on the record so that we will see the purpose behind His conversation with Abraham. He lets us know that He is not going to hide from Abraham what He is about to do. He is going to tell Abraham in advance so that Abraham will understand His ways. He needs for Abraham to understand His ways because the Lord has chosen Abraham to direct his household in the ways of the Lord. So the Lord lets Abraham in on what He is doing. Imagine how different Abraham's understanding would be if suddenly Sodom and Gomorrah were destroyed and he, Abraham, had no insight into the process.

Part of letting Abraham in on the process is letting Abraham explore the process—letting him ask the hard questions. The Lord tells Abraham His plan: "Sodom and Gomorrah have become so wicked that I will destroy them." This awakens in Abraham a response—one the Lord had expected to awaken. Abraham says, *"Will you sweep away the righteous with the wicked? What if there are fifty righteous people in the city? Will you really sweep it away and not spare the place for the sake of the fifty righteous people in it? Far be it from you to do such a thing—to kill the righteous with the wicked, treating the righteous and the wicked alike. Far be it from you! Will not the Judge of all the earth do right?"* (Genesis 18:23–25).

Now, let me ask you a couple of questions at this point. Did Abraham see things more clearly than God? Did He shame the Lord into "doing right?" Is that why God said to Abraham, *"If I find fifty righteous people in the city of Sodom, I will spare the whole place for their sake"* (Genesis 18:26). Did He reevaluate and listen to Abraham's more moderate approach?

I suggest that the dynamics were as follows: God gives Abraham a glimpse of what He is going to do in order to engage Abraham and encourage

Abraham to explore the situation with Him and so reach an understanding of God's ways. Abraham begins to voice what He knows about God: "God wouldn't treat the righteous and wicked alike. He would never do that! He is the Judge of all the earth and He will do right! I wonder if that means that for the sake of fifty righteous people He would spare the whole city? I think I'll ask Him."

God assured Abraham that if there had been as many as fifty righteous people, He would have spared the city for their sakes. God, you see, has already thought of that. He doesn't stop and consider and then say, "OK. I guess that I would save the city for fifty righteous people."

Abraham is encouraged by the Lord's responses to him to keep asking questions. Abraham learns that the Lord would have spared the city if He had found even ten righteous people in it. Because of this exchange with the Lord, when the city was destroyed, Abraham had a mature understanding of the ways of the Lord. He saw the situation through the prism of His exchange with the Lord.

I don't have the space to explore every instance when a surface glance will cause you to think God changed His mind. Each time, understand that God is presenting the situation as it will look unless God intervenes. He does this in order to engage the person and awaken a response that will open the way for God to intervene and change the course events will take on their own.

God chooses to bring His people into His activity. He chooses to work through the praying lives of His people. This does not mean that God is helpless or powerless without us. There are many things that God could do without us, but chooses not to. C. S. Lewis wrote:

Infinite wisdom does not need telling what is best, and infinite goodness needs no urging to do it. But neither does God need any of those things that are done by infinite agents, whether living or inanimate. He could, if He chose, repair our bodies miraculously without food; or give us food without the aid of farmers, bakers, and butchers; or knowledge without the aid of learned men; or convert the heathen without missionaries. Instead, He allows soils and weather and animals and muscles, minds, and wills of men to cooperate in the execution of His will. "God," said Pascal, "instituted prayer to lend to His creatures the dignity of causality."

—C. S. Lewis, in "The Efficacy of Prayer" in *The World's Last Night and Other Essays*

Five. The Spiritual Discipline of Fasting

1. Jesus expected His followers to fast. In fact, He gave specific instructions for how to fast.

"The time will come when the bridegroom will be taken from them; then they will fast." —Matthew 9:15

"When you fast, do not look somber as the hypocrites do, for they disfigure their faces to show men they are fasting. I tell you the truth, they have received their reward in full. But when you fast, put oil on your head and wash your face, so that it will not be obvious to men that you are fasting, but only to your Father, who is unseen; and your Father, who sees what is done in secret, will reward you." —Matthew 6:16–18

2. The church fasted in order to hear from God.

While they were worshiping the Lord and fasting, the Holy Spirit said, "Set apart for me Barnabas and Saul for the work to which I have called them." So after they had fasted and prayed, they placed their hands on them and sent them off. —Acts 13:2–3

3. The church fasted on behalf of their leaders and those in service.

Paul and Barnabas appointed elders for them in each church and, with prayer and fasting, committed them to the Lord, in whom they had put their trust. —Acts 14:23

4. When more power is called for, fasting is required.

He replied, "This kind can come out only by prayer and fasting."
—Mark 9:29

What can you expect to experience during a fast?
1. Hunger…your physical body needs food and is trained to expect food. You will probably experience both a physical and psychological craving for food (or for the food groups you are fasting from).

   A. Turn hunger and craving into prayer. "Father, as my body craves food, I crave Your presence."

Meanwhile his disciples urged him, "Rabbi, eat something." But he said to them, "I have food to eat that you know nothing about." Then his disciples said to each other, "Could someone have brought him food?" "My food," said Jesus, "is to do the will of him who sent me and to finish his work." —John 4:31–34

B. Your hunger and food-craving will remind you to turn to God and to keep your mind stayed on Him. Consider hunger a positive feeling because it will turn your heart to the Father.

"I have treasured the words of his mouth more than my daily bread."
—Job 23:12

C. Hunger and food-cravings will give you the opportunity to present an offering to the Lord. Each time you deny your craving for the sake of your fast, you are placing a sacrifice on the altar. The offering is not the food, but your obedience.

2. Crucifixion moments…God is always in the process of breaking the power of your flesh (human nature disconnected from the Spirit's power). During a fast, as the Spirit of God sensitizes you to spiritual things, you may be confronted over and over again with your flesh's primary sin-patterns.

A. Recognize these moments for what they are: God's doing, not Satan's.

B. Recognize what God is revealing: the root of unrighteousness in your flesh that continues to grow a fruit called sin.

C. Be aware of the potential in these moments: to be progressively freed from attitudes that have long bound you.

D. Act on God's provision for these moments: flesh **must** submit to Spirit. (Read Romans 8:2.) For a more extensive look at "crucifixion moments," read *He Restores My Soul: A Forty-Day Journey Toward Personal Renewal*.

3. An increasing desire for the things of God. God will begin to create in you a spiritual craving that only He can satisfy. In this way, He will draw you deeper and deeper into the Spirit's life.

4. An increasing awareness of the Spirit of God in you. You will find yourself putting less and less confidence in your flesh. In fact, you will become so aware of the emptiness and foolishness of your flesh that you will cry out to God day and night to expose your flesh and crucify it.

What should I do during a fast?

1. Set aside a daily extended time for prayer and listening to God. If you are fasting a certain meal, consider making that mealtime your prayer time.

2. Keep a journal.

3. Consider partnering with someone for accountability, encouragement, and sharing thoughts.

Six. The Power of Agreement

"Again, I tell you that if two of you on earth agree about anything you ask for, it will be done for you by my Father in heaven. For where two or three come together in my name, there am I with them." —Matthew 18:19–20

Jesus teaches us that there is power in agreeing prayer. As we ask the Spirit to lead us into all truth about agreeing prayer, ask Him to teach us the answers to these questions:

1. What does it mean to agree?
2. With whom must we agree?
3. How do we "come together in [His] name"?
4. Does Jesus arrive because two or three are gathered, or is He already within each believer?

The unified prayers of the church govern the spiritual world.

His intent was that now, through the church, the manifold wisdom of God should be made known to the rulers and authorities in the heavenly realms. —Ephesians 3:10

**The measure of the power of the church today determines the measure of the manifestation of the power of God. For His power is now revealed through the church. This whole matter can be likened to the flow of water in one's house. Though the water tank of the Water Supply Company is huge, its flow is limited to the diameter of the water pipe in one's own house. If a person wishes to have more flow of water, he will need to enlarge his water pipe. Today the degree of the manifestation of God's power is governed by the capacity of the church.
—Watchman Nee,** *The Prayer Ministry of the Church*

It is both sobering and astounding to realize that God has chosen to express Himself on earth through His church. We are the pipeline through which the power of God flows. The size of His power is infinite; the flow of His power is limited only by our capacity to receive it.

The prayers of the church announce to the powers, principalities, and authorities of the spiritual realm what God's wisdom is. The spiritual realm must deploy accordingly. When the church, through prayer, announces God's Word (will), Satan's forces must back down and the forces of God must carry out His Word. The gates of hell cannot stand against the onslaught of the church.

However, there are conditions that must be in place before this kind of authority goes into effect.

The church must pray in agreement.

The power of unity is a universal principle, not just a church-principle. People working together toward an agreed-upon goal are all but unstoppable. Early in the history of humankind, God stated this truth.

Now the whole world had one language and a common speech. As men moved eastward, they found a plain in Shinar and settled there. They said to each other, "Come, let's make bricks and bake them thoroughly.' They used brick instead of stone, and tar for mortar. Then they said, 'Come, let us build ourselves a city, with a tower that reaches to the heavens, so that we may make a name for ourselves and not be scattered over the face of the whole earth.' But the LORD came down to see the city and the tower that the men were building. The LORD said, 'If as one people speaking the same language they have begun to do this, then **nothing they plan to do will be impossible for them**.*"* —Genesis 11:1–6*

God had to disrupt unity and divide the human race in order to stop them from bringing destruction. The power of their unity was so great that God Himself declared that *"nothing they plan to do will be impossible for them."* Humankind was unified for a purpose—a purpose that would bring disaster on the earth. God had to scatter the human race until the day when He could reverse the division and restore unity—until the day when He, by His indwelling Spirit, could bring humans into agreement with Him and, finally, with each other. The unity described in Genesis was dangerous because humans were in agreement with *each other*, but not in agreement *with God*.

How did God disrupt their unity?

The LORD said, "If as one people **speaking the same language** *they have begun to do this, then nothing they plan to do will be impossible for them. Come, let us go down and* **confuse their language** *so they will not understand each other." So the LORD scattered them from there over all the earth, and they stopped building the city. That is why it was called Babel—because there the LORD confused the language of the whole world. From there the LORD scattered them over the face of the whole earth.* —Genesis 11:6–10

God confused their language so that when they spoke, they did not understand each other. On the day of Pentecost, He reversed what He had done. On the day that the Holy Spirit came to indwell believers, on the day that God took up residence in the spirits of His people, on that day He restored unity. On that day, no matter what language a person spoke, each understood it as if it were spoken in his own language.

When the day of Pentecost came, they were all together in one place. Suddenly a sound like the blowing of a violent wind came from heaven and filled the whole house where they were sitting. They saw what seemed to be tongues of fire that separated and came to rest on each of them. All of them were filled with the Holy Spirit and began to speak in other tongues as the Spirit enabled them. Now there were staying in Jerusalem God-fearing Jews from every nation under heaven. When they heard this sound, a crowd came together in bewilderment, because **each one heard them speaking in his own language**. *Utterly amazed, they asked: "Are not all these men who are speaking Galileans? Then how is it that each of us hears them in his own native language? Parthians, Medes and Elamites; residents of Mesopotamia, Judea and Cappadocia, Pontus and Asia, Phrygia and Pamphylia, Egypt and the parts of Libya near Cyrene; visitors from Rome (both Jews and converts to Judaism); Cretans and Arabs—we hear them declaring the wonders of God in our own tongues!" Amazed and perplexed, they asked one another, "What does this mean?"* —Acts 2:1–12

In Genesis, God caused mankind to be unable to understand each other. In Acts, He caused them to understand each other, no matter the native language of the hearer. He restored their unity so that "nothing they plan to do will be impossible for them."

What is spiritual agreement?

Spiritual agreement is something different from having the same opinion. It goes much deeper. Agreement among believers begins in the heart of each individual believer before God. It's a simple matter to find someone who "agrees" with you—someone who has the same opinion of what God should do in any given matter. This kind of agreement, in fact, weakens prayer. Why? Because two people who are drawn together because they have the same opinion will strengthen that opinion in each other. These two people will feed each other's "arguments and pretensions" and will actually keep each other from hearing from God. Opinions about how God should handle a certain matter are **always** dangerous. A pray-er who is listening to God can know what God wants to do but not how He is going to do it. He wants to *"fill you with the knowledge of his will through all spiritual wisdom and understanding"* (Colossians 1:9), but *"his paths [are] beyond tracing out"* (Romans 11:33).

As believers, we have strongholds. Strongholds, as referred to in 2 Corinthians 10:4, are fortresses. Fortresses are erected to defend or protect something within their walls. These fortresses, Scripture says, are built out of arguments and pretensions. Arguments and pretensions serve to protect lies and stubborn opinions.

For though we live in the world, we do not wage war as the world does. The weapons we fight with are not the weapons of the world. On the contrary, they have divine power to demolish strongholds. We demolish arguments and every pretension that sets itself up against the knowledge of God, and we take captive every thought to make it obedient to Christ. —2 Corinthians 10:3–5

"The weapons we fight with" are prayers—words initiated by God and voiced by believers. We don't tear down strongholds with brute force or our bare hands. We don't tear down strongholds with arguments and reasoning. We tear them down with prayer. When we allow strongholds to exist and protect our favorite opinions, we cannot hear God's voice. How can you know if you have a stronghold protecting an opinion or an attitude? By how many arguments you need to support and justify it!

So you can see that if two people who have erected strongholds to protect the same opinion come together, the result will not be the tearing down of strongholds, but the strengthening of strongholds. When two people of the same opinion come together to give God instructions about how to work out a situation, there will be **no spiritual power**. This is not agreeing in prayer; this is ganging up on God!

To pray with power, the pray-er must agree with God.
"Again, I tell you that if two of you on earth agree about anything you ask for, it will be done for you by my Father in heaven. For where two or three come together in my name, there am I with them." —Matthew 18:19–20

What does it mean, then, to agree in prayer? The word translated *agree* is a word from which we get the English word *symphony*. It means to harmonize, to blend several voices into one. The word *agree* means to be in harmony, but not necessarily in unison.

With whom must a pray-er agree? He must agree with God. A pray-er must be in agreement with the intercession of Jesus, who is always in agreement with the will of God. When more than one intercessor, each of whom is in agreement with God, come together to pray God's will, then anything they ask Him to do, He will do.

"Where two or three come together in [His] name." Concerted intercession produces effects on the earth. The word translated *come together* is the Greek word *sunago*, which means to join together; to make one. It is the composite of two words: *sun*, which means to bring into complete union, and *ago*, which means to lead, guide, or induce. The verb is in the passive

tense, which means that the subject (two or three intercessors) is acted upon. They do not come together on their own initiative, but are brought together. They are led into complete union.

Agreeing intercessors, then, are joined together by His power acting on them. These intercessors come together "in [His] name." The Greek is more correctly translated "into His name." These intercessors are drawn into the power of His name. When they are joined together into His name, "there [He] is with them." The word translated *with them* is a Greek word (*mesos*) that really means *among*. It implies dispersion and intermixture. In other words, He is the solvent in which the intercessors' lives have become one.

Jesus is not absent until two or three come together. Instead, He is present in the lives of each individual intercessor so that when they come together, He is within and among them. When the wills of two or more intercessors are immersed and dissolved in His perfect will, every single thing they ask will be done by the Father.

Increased spiritual power is released when the church prays in agreement.
When we, the church, learn how to agree in prayer, the power of God is multiplied on the earth. The same principle is in effect as was in effect in Genesis: "If as one people speaking the same language they have begun to do this, then nothing they plan to do will be impossible for them." When we are unified through the Spirit, we are "speaking the same language."

Jesus gave us the language to use to pray in agreement with Him: "Let Your kingdom come and let Your will be done on earth in the same way Your will is done in heaven."

A Message from Jennifer Kennedy Dean

PRAYER IS THE KEY TO EVERYTHING. What God wants to do on the earth, He does through prayer. Prayer is so much more than the words that come sandwiched between "Dear God" and "Amen." We limit prayer's power by our misconceptions about what prayer is. My heart-passion is to teach others the deep truths about prayer that the Father is teaching me.

Many believers are secretly discouraged about prayer. Many have reached the conclusion that prayer only works for "other people" or that prayer is, at best, a hit-or-miss activity. Yet the Scripture says that God intends for prayer to be the conduit that brings His power out of the spiritual realm and causes it to show up on the earth. The Scripture says that the prayer of one righteous person will exercise force and produce results on earth. God makes astonishing claims about prayer's power. Why aren't we living in that power?

The ministry of the Praying Life Foundation is to point God's people to His Word to find what makes prayer work the way He intends for it to work. We know there is only one Prayer Teacher. My goal is to be a vessel through which He can teach.

I don't know about you, but I cannot be satisfied with a trickle when I know there's a river to be had. I am always seeking to go deeper in the life of the Spirit. Through books and seminars, I share my journey with those who share my hunger.

Jennifer Kennedy Dean

BLESSED ARE THOSE...
WHO HAVE SET
THEIR HEARTS
ON PILGRIMAGE

[PSALM 84:5]

TO SCHEDULE
Jennifer Kennedy Dean
FOR YOUR EVENT, CONTACT:

The Praying Life Foundation
P. O. Box 660
Marion, KY 42064

seminars@prayinglife.org
www.prayinglife.org

Visit www.prayinglife.org to:

- Find answers to frequently asked questions
- Ask Jennifer your own questions
- Find a monthly column by Jennifer Kennedy Dean
- Discover a wealth of resources for your praying life

Books by Jennifer Kennedy Dean

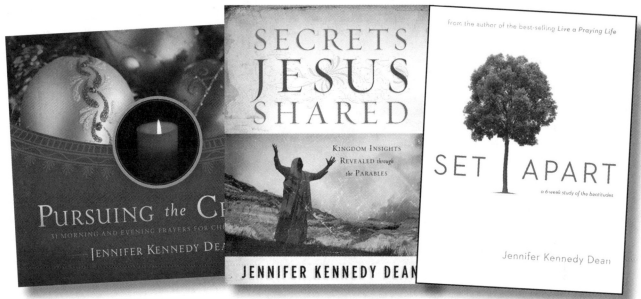

Pursuing the Christ
*31 Morning and Evening
Prayers for Christmastime*
ISBN-10: 1-59669-320-7
ISBN-13: 978-1-59669-320-3

Secrets Jesus Shared
*Kingdom Insights Revealed
through the Parables*
ISBN-10: 1-59669-108-5
ISBN-13: 978-1-59669-108-7

Set Apart
*A 6-Week Study
of the Beatitudes*
ISBN-10: 1-59669-263-4
ISBN-13: 978-1-59669-263-3

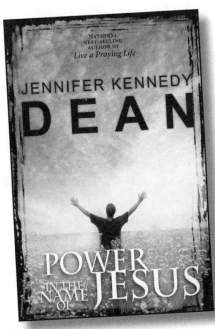

Power in the Name of Jesus
ISBN-10: 1-59669-356-8
ISBN-13: 978-1-59669-356-2

Life Unhindered!
Five Keys to Walking in Freedom
ISBN-10: 1-59669-286-3
ISBN-13: 978-1-59669-286-2

Heart's Cry
Principles of Prayer
ISBN-10: 1-59669-412-2
ISBN-13: 978-1-59669-412-5

For information about these books or any New Hope product,
visit www.newhopepublishers.com.

Available in bookstores everywhere.

New Hope® Publishers is a division of WMU®, an international organization that challenges Christian believers to understand and be radically involved in God's mission. For more information about WMU, go to www.wmu.com. More information about New Hope books may be found at www.newhopepublishers.com. New Hope books may be purchased at your local bookstore.

If you've been blessed by this book, we would like to hear your story. The publisher and author welcome your comments and suggestions at: newhopereader@wmu.org.